VIKI

THE LAST HEROES

PALAGUMMI SAINATH is founder-editor of the People's Archive of Rural India (PARI). He has been a journalist and reporter for forty-two years, covering rural India full-time for thirty of those. With an MA in History from JNU, Sainath joined the United News of India in 1980. In 1982, he became foreign editor of *The Daily* and deputy chief editor of the weekly *Blitz* in Mumbai. In 1993, he left *Blitz* to work full-time on reporting rural poverty. He was rural affairs editor of *The Hindu* from 2004 to 2014.

Sainath has won over 60 national and international reporting awards and fellowships. These include the Fukuoka Grand Prize 2021, the World Media Summit Award 2014, the Ramon Magsaysay Award in 2007, Amnesty International's Global Human Rights Reporting Prize and the Ramnath Goenka Journalist of the Year award. He has been teaching journalism at the Sophia Polytechnic, Mumbai, for three decades, and also at the Asian College of Journalism, Chennai, since 2000. He was McGraw Professor of Writing in Princeton in 2012.

In December 2014, Sainath launched PARI. Publishing in 14 languages, PARI is an independent multimedia digital platform, whose reporting mandate is to cover every region and section of rural people. In seven years, PARI has won over 50 journalism awards.

Sainath lives in Mumbai.

THE LAST HEROES

Foot Soldiers
of INDIAN
FREEDOM

P. SAINATH

PENGUIN
VIKING

An imprint of Penguin Random House

VIKING

USA | Canada | UK | Ireland | Australia
New Zealand | India | South Africa | China

Viking is part of the Penguin Random House group of companies
whose addresses can be found at global.penguinrandomhouse.com

Published by Penguin Random House India Pvt. Ltd
4th Floor, Capital Tower 1, MG Road,
Gurugram 122 002, Haryana, India

First published in Viking by Penguin Random House India 2022

ISBN 9780670096923

Typeset in Adobe Garamond Pro by Manipal Technologies Limited, Manipal
Printed at Replika Press Pvt. Ltd, India

www.penguin.co.in

'We fought for two things—for Freedom and Independence. We attained Independence.'

—'Captain Bhau', Ramchandra Sripati Lad,
Leader of the Toofan Sena
Kundal, Sangli, Maharashtra

For my mother,
whose stories of freedom fighters I grew up on,
including those of her father
who spent years in British jails

CONTENTS

Contents

THE SPIRIT OF INDIAN FREEDOM @75

PROFESSOR JAGMOHAN

We are in the seventy-fifth year of our Independence from British colonialism. The freedom movement that brought us an independent nation created a culture of determination, dedication and selfless service that percolated deep into the people. It inspired millions upon millions of men and women to face unbelievable odds with a smile. To know how the commoners, ordinary people, took this culture into their lives is to know the spirit of the freedom struggle.

And nothing is more exciting than to listen to the few yet surviving persons of that era tell us their stories. So, the tales of the freedom fighters in this book make it a precious work and a gift to the Azadi ka Amrit Mahotsav.

In the achievement of Independence, a large part of the population contributed in diverse ways. Everything changed with their entry into the struggle. As Bhagat Singh noted, a new era began when Gandhi brought the energies of commoners into the freedom struggle. He wrote in a letter of 2 February

1931, 'In a sense Gandhism . . . makes a nearer approach to the revolutionary ideas. For it counts on mass action, though not for the masses alone . . . The Revolutionary must give to the angel of non-violence his due.'

It is a matter of concern that our current generations are fast losing their links to the culture of the freedom struggle. They are restless and confused because they are unaware and kept uninformed of the social values capable of contributing to the progress of society. Because they are not conscious of the historical experience of commoners which contributed so much to that achievement whose seventy-fifth year we now celebrate.

Maybe this problem arises in narrating history only through famous personalities and forgetting the role of the subaltern. There is even a strong tendency to view history as one of rajas and ranis only, as if the struggles of commoners were non-existent. That is why this generation is left feeling helpless, frustrated and confused.

The effort in this book of looking at the role of ordinary people reminds me of a dialogue between Bhagat Singh and his compatriot Shiv Verma, which went as follows:

We, as soldiers of freedom, love action, and in the action the most honoured are those who either achieve martyrdom in the field or at the gallows. But they are nothing but the gems on the top of a building. They only enhance the beauty of the building. But the stones which make the foundation are much more important. They strengthen the foundation and provide long life to the building. It is they who carry the burden for many long years.

What better appreciation of the importance of the foot soldiers of freedom! So this presentation of the stories of such people, those basic stones of the foundation, is very valuable.

In the 1960s, I had the privilege of meeting the old Ghadar party heroes of the 1914–15 uprising. These were people who had migrated to America, Canada and elsewhere to save their families from the impoverishment created by famines and pandemics under colonial rule. They did much better there— yet they returned en masse to India, having learnt of the sufferings their compatriots faced. They believed they could never be free while their fellow Indians remained slaves to British imperialism.

To fight against the Empire, they saw the need to have dedicated volunteers. Those volunteers would commit to serve the people with full devotion and with no expectation of reward or returns. They would help people to understand the cause of their troubles. Once the cause was understood, the solution would follow.

Many were hanged to death by the British. Most of the rest were incarcerated for long periods. Brutal prison time did not dim their enthusiasm, though. Once out of jail, they took up causes such as helping establish schools for girls and boys who had no access to education. Once, I set out in search of Baba Hari Singh Usman, a Ghadari of the 1914–15 uprising, who later served in establishing the Indian National Army (INA) under Netaji Subhas Bose. He had returned to India in 1946. I found him at the construction site of a village school.

I asked him how he was out at the school site in such hot weather at his advanced age. His reply: 'It was the conviction of our party that the important revolutionary work is to ensure education of the younger generation.' That attitude inspired many of us youths to silently perform our basic duty towards our fellow human beings. There is a lot for us to learn from that generation.

But when we realized that there were so many like him in the villages, the first thought that struck me was how badly we as a society were neglecting them. And so, were failing to learn from those with a history of long suffering behind them during the freedom struggle. They were also a group facing callous official neglect. What a way to kill the idea of sacrifice for social progress! It was planned that these soldiers of freedom be taken to the schools and colleges to interact with young people. It happened for a while and had a very salutary effect on the youth. The process died out, however.

Why did that happen? Was it by design that they were kept away from public sight? I think, reading *Lawley Road* by R. K. Narayan, that the answer is yes.* More so when a class of people

---

* *Lawley Road* is set in Malgudi. In the weeks following Independence, as the local municipality scrambles to honour the freedom fighters and celebrate the nation's newfound Independence, a series of darkly comic events ensue—local representatives fighting with each other to name roads in their wards after Gandhi, Nehru and others; the bringing

who were turncoats happen to be in power. It also makes one understand why it took many years to get some great movements of the freedom struggle recognized officially. Is it that the colonial 'steel frame', which was kept intact post-Independence, became a strangulating hand to crush the notion of freedom?

I remember some of our own relatives who were pro-British during the freedom struggle. They would, after Independence, visit my mother, pursuing personal favours. This was for the first thirty to forty years after 1947. Later, they were back in positions of power and would never visit. In the early post-Independence period, they lay low, fearing that their properties gained by acting against the struggle and collaborating with British colonial rulers might be confiscated. The system was manipulated to favour these resourceful persons. There was a time when, in elections, voters chose people who had given themselves to public service. Then slowly, that changed to favour those with property and resources. The *Lawley Road* turncoat class was influential and began to get a grip on independent India.

There was a time when there were efforts and events to provide recognition to those who contributed to the fight for Independence. But I personally know how difficult it was for the freedom fighters to meet bureaucratic formalities. The

---

down of a statue of a Britisher misidentified as being a tyrant (turns out he was extremely good to Indians); and the shenanigans of a Chairman who seeks to mask his previous record as someone who did nothing for the town and actually favoured the British. Through token gestures (like the ones named here), he attempts to stay on as Chairman.

jail records have only the British version of everything. The Raj never wanted the people of the struggle to be known for their commitment to freedom. Fabricated cases were created to not only punish them but to break their souls. In most cases, land or property confiscated from freedom fighters was never restored.

Nations that value the spirit of freedom have made all efforts to preserve the artifacts and stories of commoners to help inculcate those values into their new generations.

A plea to build a memorial of the struggles for freedom from 1757 to 1947 was finally silently scotched by building a war memorial—post Independence. It looks like the legacy of selfless dedication that prevailed during the struggle in those long years is to be expunged from our history.

Bhagat Singh's uncle Ajit Singh and his compatriot Sufi Amba Parshad, while leaving India to build support for the freedom movement amongst immigrant Indians, left a great message in a speech on 11 July 1909. It was titled 'How Nations Progress and How Nations Fall'. Narrating examples from the history of great empires that had fallen, they concluded that the lesson to be learnt was this: If the sense of freedom and unity prevails amongst its people, then the nation progresses. But if the people are divided on the basis of nationality, religion or caste, and if hatred against each other is propagated, that is a sure symptom of a coming fall.

In seventy-five years, we seem to have reduced 'Independence' to mean that the ruling elites are independent to take decisions.

How rich are those words of Rabindranath Tagore in his essay 'The Spirit of Freedom', after his third visit to America in 1920. He wrote: 'When freedom is not an inner idea which imparts strength to our activities and breadth to our creations, when it is merely a thing of external circumstance, it is like an open space to one who is blindfolded.'

Now a few words about this wonderful book by P. Sainath.

This is a marvellous work done consistently over years to collect the stories of living freedom fighters. They survived and waited for someone to come to not only listen to their stories but share them with the world as a part of our history.

These stories were reported from all over India by Sainath, and they are from various regions, cultures and backgrounds. They should convince us of how deep and widespread was the longing for freedom in our great struggle. Let it be appreciated that behind the achievement of Independence, there lay so much sacrifice, suffering and dedication. Some of them may have fallen victim to bureaucratic apathy, but it is our duty as a society to keep their values alive. In a time when more emphasis is given to building tall statues, I'm reminded of an old saying: 'If one takes away the spirit, one is left with a statue.'

Let the current generations remember that now we may have Independence, but the essence of freedom is lacking. Let these stories where living fighters speak explain what that was. The people in this book are real freedom fighters—not dependent on official records or certificates.

Bhagat Singh and B. K. Dutta wrote in a letter to the editor, *Modern Review*, on 24 December 1929:

It is the lethargic spirit that needs to be replaced by the revolutionary spirit. Otherwise degeneration gains the upper hand and the whole humanity is led astray by the reactionary forces. Such a state of affairs leads to stagnation and paralysis in human progress. The spirit of Revolution should always permeate the soul of humanity, so that the reactionary forces may not accumulate [strength] to check its eternal onward march. The old order should change, always and ever, yielding place to the new, so that one 'good' order may not corrupt the world. It is in this sense that we raise the shout *Inqilab Zindabad* [Long Live the Revolution].

This collection of spellbinding accounts of the freedom fighters based on extensive interviews with them, and their families, allows us to appreciate each one of them. Sainath's book is a great idea and effort and excellent storytelling. A gift in the seventy-fifth year of our Independence.

I thank and congratulate Sainath on this effort, which can be seen as an Ordinary People's History of the Freedom Struggle. A book that can rekindle the idea and essence of freedom most needed in our present times.

I strongly recommend this book to our younger generations, to carefully study and absorb. You should search around and see, you may have a story in your family too.

Jagmohan
Ludhiana

Professor Jagmohan Singh, 78, is the nephew of India's most famous freedom fighter and revolutionary—the legendary Bhagat Singh. His mother Bibi Amar Kaur was Shaheed Bhagat Singh's younger sister. Professor Jagmohan spent about nine months in Ambala Central Jail in 1945–46—at age one and a half! His mother had been jailed for making bold speeches against British imperialism and also for criticizing their Indian lackeys.

Only much later would he get to learn from his mother that many other prisoners used to come and play with him. And that some of those were, in fact, members of Netaji Subhas Chandra Bose's INA.

Very early in life, Bibi Amar Kaur impressed on her son that it was his duty and responsibility to help people everywhere understand Bhagat Singh better.

Professor Jagmohan is an alumnus of IIT Kharagpur and retired as the Head of Computer Sciences at Punjab Agricultural University, Ludhiana.

INTRODUCTION

WHO WERE OUR FREEDOM FIGHTERS?

'Great men seem to be the cause of revolutions in the world.
In truth, the people themselves are the cause.'

—M. K. Gandhi, 17 January 1931
Letter from Yerawada Central Jail

Demati Dei Sabar 'Salihan' was not a freedom fighter. Not to the government of India, anyway. Yet, when barely sixteen, this Adivasi girl led a spectacular counterattack on a British police force raiding her village in Odisha. She and forty other young tribal women took on a platoon of armed police with only lathis—and won.

She did not go to jail. She was not a part of organized politics. She had no role in campaigns like the Civil Disobedience or Quit India movements. In the village of Saliha, where she led that death-defying charge, they still speak of her valour. In the same village, the names of seventeen people are inscribed on a monument to the uprising. Her name is not among them.

The government of India would never accord Salihan respect as a freedom fighter.

This book does.

In the next five or six years, there will not be a single person alive who fought for this country's freedom. The youngest of those featured in this book is 92, the oldest 104. Newer generations of young Indians will never get to meet, see, speak or listen to India's freedom fighters. Never be directly told who they were, what they fought for.

In the seventy-fifth year of Indian Independence, most books, especially those for younger people, mainly focus on the names of a few select individuals as having brought this nation into being. There are still some fine textbooks around that do look at the struggle for freedom and Independence in a sensible and explanatory way. But those are being savaged and rapidly replaced in state after state with appalling fabrications that don't qualify as history, let alone as textbooks.

In the political and public domain today, the freedom struggle itself is being dated back 800 years. That kind of retelling of India's fight for freedom gives fiction a bad name. Meanwhile, those who fought for that freedom are vanishing. As many as six of those who feature in this book have died since May 2021. But some of the others whose stories appear here are very much alive and around. Sadly, that can't be for more than a few years. With the exception perhaps of Mallu

Swarajyam and H. S. Doreswamy, these fighters have not featured as major characters in any books. Certainly not in schoolbooks, or in books for a young generation set to lose a national treasure.

There are over 23,000 names on the Union government's 'Name-wise and State-wise list of Freedom Fighters and eligible dependents' as of 31 January 2022. It's a record of those drawing pensions under the Swatantrata Sainik Samman Yojana (SSSY). Amounts not exceeding Rs 30,000 a month are paid out to accounts in these names. Many more figure on the pension lists of the states and union territories.

Statutory warning: Annoying and arcane bureaucratic details ahead.

It is important to understand that the official lists of freedom fighters are woefully incomplete. And since we all know that reading the fine print of the government of India's rules is injurious to your health, let's just look at a few of the details.

For one thing, most of the people *originally* on all these lists are no longer alive. Many of the names there now are, in fact, those of dependents, where the freedom fighter has long since passed. The families of the fighters are entitled in several cases to half that pension as 'eligible dependents'. That is a good thing—but muddies the numbers of the actual freedom fighters on the lists. (Most of those still alive are also infirm and inarticulate.)

Secondly, very large groups of those who fought for freedom do not appear on the official lists. In 1972, when the first such pension scheme began, the Left parties decided their members would not accept these. As one of them, N. Sankariah, says in this book, 'We fought for freedom, not for pensions.'

That means thousands and thousands of fighters never appeared on the lists. It's worth remembering there were a lot more such individuals alive in 1972. Also, that the list then was most restrictive. Only those earning less than Rs 5,000 a year were eligible. And the pension was all of Rs 200 a month.

The Swatantrata Sainik Samman scheme of 1980 was more generous.* However, the first of the 'eligible' categories demands the fighter must 'have suffered minimum imprisonment of six months in mainland jails before Independence'. For women, Dalits and Adivasis, that was made three months.

That again excluded several who may have escaped incarceration (unless they qualified under one of six other criteria). Or who did not serve three to six months in jail. It also excludes many more in the revolutionary underground movements who did not go to prison.

As Laxmi Panda (see Chapter 9)—the Odia woman who joined Netaji Bose's Indian National Army—asked me, 'Because I never went to jail, because I trained with a rifle

---

* Those interested in exploring the official Swatantrata Sainik Samman Yojana and the Union government's freedom fighters' pensioners list, please refer to the following websites: https://www.mha.gov.in/sites/default/files/Annexure%201.pdf; https://www.mha.gov.in/sites/default/files/UpdatedlistofSSSYBeneficiaries_04022022.pdf.

but never fired a bullet at anyone, does that mean I am not a freedom fighter? I only worked in INA forest camps that were targets of British bombing. Does that mean I made no contribution to the freedom struggle? At thirteen, I was cooking in the camp kitchens for all those who were going out and fighting, was I not part of that?'

In fact, those who *volunteered* to fight underground are *not* eligible. As one note in the scheme document states, 'Voluntary underground suffering or self-exile and suffering for party work under the command of party leadership are specifically ineligible for grant of pension.'

The pension was extended only to those who went underground as a result of their being proclaimed offenders by the British Raj. Or if they had a detention order against them. Or if there was an award for their arrest or head. That rules out Laxmi Panda, Salihan and countless others like them.

There's another problem with the 1980 scheme document. It uses the word 'widow' rather than a term like 'spouse'. Which seems to presume freedom fighters were only men.

And there is also the question of what we as a society believe qualifies as 'participation' in the freedom struggle. Of those we have never thought of as freedom fighters. Under the central scheme, 'participation' isn't enough. The person must have 'suffered'—and only in ways defined by the government.

The Seven Laws of Suffering as understood by officialdom: Imprisonment. Driven underground on being proclaimed an offender. Internment/externment. Or having your property confiscated, attached or sold. (What about those who owned no property in the first place?)

Further: Losing your government job. (Again, this could have excluded many who did a great deal while retaining their jobs.) Or if you were permanently incapacitated. Or if you suffered ten strokes of caning, whipping or flogging.

The proof of eligibility required is another mess. Another story. Its first demand is a copy of the order of your arrest. Or of your being proclaimed an offender. How many poor Indians could ever have accessed such records even at that time, let alone twenty-five years after Independence? How many poor Indians underwent arbitrary detention without any such orders being passed?

There were thousands whose role in the struggle entailed suffering other than those mandated by the Act. Many took incredible risks and suffered in other ways. Most victories would have been impossible without them. But their activity, often seen as lowly, did not render them worthy of being 'freedom fighters' in official eyes.

As all the fighters whose stories you find here assure us, it was the recognition that mattered, not so much the money. The money matters, too. But they think it's not half as important as having their nation cherish them. And having us recognize the role that ordinary people played in India's epic struggle for freedom and Independence.

Many of them do need that money and, certainly, the recognition. The rest of us, the post-1947 generations—*we need their stories*. To better shape our own. To learn what they understood. That Freedom and Independence are not the same thing. To learn to make those coalesce.

In this book are people who were farmers, landless labourers, workers, couriers, forest produce gatherers, homemakers, domestic help. There are even a couple of rebel members from families of landed gentry. In one village the British called the Badmash Gaon, there were carpenters, leather workers and others.

Sometimes, it's worth listening to the history of that great struggle as understood by those who helped make it. Not one of the people in this book became or sought to be Ministers, Governors, Prime Ministers or Presidents after 1947. One, though, served briefly as a reluctant and maverick MLA in Andhra Pradesh.

The stories in this book were done over many years and multiple interviews. Among the people in it are Adivasis, Dalits, OBCs, Brahmins, Muslims, Hindus and Sikhs. Also, women, men and very young children (many of these fighters were active even before they entered their teens). They spoke or speak different languages. They are from different rural regions, cultures and backgrounds. They include atheists and believers.

They had this in common, though: Their opposition to Empire was uncompromising. They were aware of the risks they were taking. They had a vision, an idea, of the freedom they were seeking. They never stoked or drummed up hatred against 'other' communities. They fought the British Raj, not their fellow Indians. When imprisoned, they did not spend their time whining, whinging or writing pitiful mercy petitions to the British monarch, promising to be collaborators.

A few of these stories were first published in much shorter form in *The Hindu*. Some more, in the People's Archive of Rural India (PARI). In this book, those have been majorly redone with return visits to the villages of the fighters over twenty years. Some of these now include conversations with the descendants of those freedom fighters, such as Salihan, who have passed. All the stories are based on long conversations with the fighters themselves. Also, with their slightly younger friends and relatives. With the people of their villages. With historians of that era. And on some records and books of the processes and events the fighters were caught up in.

So who brought us Independence? I use that word 'independence', mindful of the point made by 'Captain Bhau' in this book. He said: 'We fought for Freedom and Independence. We achieved Independence.'

In August 1914, Gandhi was given a congratulatory reception in London following the success of the struggles he had led in South Africa. He shrank, however, from accepting credit for those achievements. He ascribed them, instead, to the thousands of ordinary Indians there, including indentured labourers. And to the support from other ordinary people within India. These were people, he said, 'who went into the battle with simple faith, with no thought of appreciation'.

I'd like to think the people in this book are much like those he described in that London speech, well over a century before our seventy-fifth year of Independence.

'These men and women,' he said, 'are the salt of India; on them will be built the Indian nation that is to be. We are poor mortals before these heroes and heroines.'

The QR Code at the end of each chapter leads to a collection of photos and videos of the individual in that story located in the Freedom Fighters Gallery on the People's Archive of Rural India (PARI).

1

REBEL, ACTOR, SOLDIER, SPY

THE HEROISM OF HAUSABAI

'I was not yet 4 and my aunt was 9 when they seized our farm—how much could we young ones do? We couldn't work like the grownups. So we would labour a little bit and then rest a while in the shade.'

—Hausabai Patil,
Vita, Sangli, Maharashtra

It did not matter to him that he was attacking his wife in front of a police station. Hausabai Patil's drunken husband began thrashing her mercilessly. 'My back started to ache with all the beatings,' she recalls. 'This was in front of the small police station at Bhavani Nagar in Sangli.' Only two of the station's four policemen were present. 'The other two had gone out to lunch.' Then her inebriated husband picked up a large stone. '"Now I will kill you right here with this stone," he roared.'

That brought the two policemen inside the station, till then looking on with indifference, rushing out. A woman being beaten by her husband in public was okay with them. But having to explain a murder right in front of their station could prove embarrassing.

'They tried to defuse our fight.' At this point, Hausabai was begging her brother, also present at the scene, not to make her return to her abusive husband's home. 'I said I won't go, I won't. I will stay here; you give me a small space next to your house. Instead of going with my husband to a sure death, I will stay here and survive on whatever I get . . . I don't want to suffer his beatings anymore.' But her brother turned down her pleas.

The policemen counselled the couple at length and scolded both of them severely. Finally, they brokered some kind of reconciliation between husband and wife and escorted the two to the railway station. 'Go home to your village,' they commanded the pair, fed up with the drama. But the couple protested that they had no money for a train journey. The police solved that problem and put them on a train to their village. 'They even got us tickets—I don't know if they paid for them—and put them in my hand. They told my husband— now if you want your wife to be with you, treat her properly, take care of her. Don't fight.'

The cops were to return to a very different kind of spat. One which allowed for no reconciliation. In their absence, Hausabai's comrades had looted the police station, picking up the four rifles and ammunition kept there; the very reason why she and her fake 'husband' and 'brother' had staged the literally painful drama to distract the cops.

That was in 1943. She was 17, married three years and with a young baby, Vilas, whom she left behind with an aunt when out on anti-British Raj missions.

Hausabai says she is still annoyed, nearly seventy-four years later, with the fake husband for beating her so hard to make their fight appear genuine. 'It really hurt,' she complains, but laughs as she says so. 'I kept telling him he was hitting me too hard. He said it should all look authentic, as that was the only way to bring the policemen out.' Now 91, she is telling us her story in Vita village, in Maharashtra's Sangli district, in June 2017. 'My eyes and ears pose a challenge for me (at this age), but I will tell you everything.'

And she does, most animatedly, and with a live wire energy.

Hausabai Patil fought for this country's freedom. She and her fellow actors in that drama were part of the Toofan Sena (typhoon or whirlwind army). The Sena was the armed wing of the *prati sarkar* or provisional government of Satara that declared independence from British rule in 1943.

With its headquarters in Kundal, the *prati sarkar*—an amalgam of peasants and workers—actually functioned as a government in the nearly 600 villages under its control, where it effectively overthrew British rule. Hausabai's father, the legendary Nana Patil, headed the *prati sarkar*. Both *sarkar* and *sena* had sprung up as disillusioned offshoots of the Quit India movement of 1942. Their parallel government was seen as a legitimate authority by the people of the region under their control. Satara was then a large region that included the present-day Sangli district.

Between 1943 and 1946, Hausabai (more often called Hausa*tai*—'*tai*' being a respectful reference in Marathi to an elder sister) was part of a team of revolutionaries who attacked British trains, looted police armouries and set ablaze *dak* bungalows. In those times, *dak* bungalows served as post offices, rest houses for official travellers and even, occasionally, as makeshift courtrooms.

In 1944, she also took part in underground action in Portuguese-colonized Goa, floating across the Mandovi river atop a wooden box at midnight, accompanied by comrades who swam alongside her. But she insists, 'I did some little, small work in the freedom struggle along with G. D. Bapu Lad. I did not do anything big or great.'

Hausabai was born on 12 February 1926 and was married in 1940, when just fourteen.

'My mother died in 1929 when I was just three,' she says. 'At that time, my father was already inspired by the struggle for Independence. Earlier, too, he had been guided by the ideals of Jyotiba Phule. And, subsequently, by Mahatma Gandhi. He quit his job as a *talati* [village accountant], and joined the struggle full-time . . . The aim was to bring our own government. And to inflict great damage on the British government so we could be rid of it.'

Pic: Courtesy of family of Hausabai Patil

Hausabai Patil with her father Nana Patil (c. 1950s), who had headed
the parallel *prati sarkar* government in Satara, Maharashtra 1943–46.

Warrants were out for Nana Patil and his associates. 'They had
to do their work underground.'

Nana moved from village to village, making powerful
speeches inspiring people to revolt. The 1930s saw his deepening
involvement with the revolutionary underground in Satara,
which he soon came to lead.

'There were about 500 people with him, and they all had
warrants in their names. They all had to go into hiding.

'Many of them were under warrants for four years! They
had to work undercover. They would strike at night, tear out
railway tracks. They would not derail passenger trains, but
only goods trains carrying materials important to the Raj.'

There was a price to be paid for such audacity. The British confiscated Nana Patil's farm and property.

'After my father had got married, his father died. Then everything that belonged to my grandfather became his property. The house, farms, everything . . .

And then the government came and attached our house.' That was in 1929.

'My grandmother, me, my aunt, my two uncles, so many of us lived there. We were cooking—there was *bhakri* [bajra roti] on the griddle and brinjal being cooked—when they came and sealed the home. There was just one room, ten feet by ten feet, left for us to live in.' The British also confiscated the family farm, depriving them of any source of income.

'So we thought we would do some *rojgar* [work] for others.' But people were too scared to help. The most popular resident of village Yede Machchhindra, now in Maharashtra's Sangli district, had been made an example of.

'The villagers would not talk to us. The grocer would not even give us salt. He would say, "No, I cannot give you anything. Get it from somewhere else." Sometimes we would go to other households for grinding or pounding grain. Even if they didn't call us, we would go, in the hope of getting something to eat at night. Sometimes we would get *umbryachya dodya* [fruit of the *Ficus racemosa* or Indian fig tree] and cook it to make a curry.'

On one thing, however, the villagers, fearful though they were, would not oblige the British Raj. They boycotted the auctions of Nana Patil's properties.

'Every morning and evening there would be a *dawandi*—a village crier—who would call out: "Nana Patil's farm is to be auctioned." But people would say, "Why should we take over Nana's farm? He has neither robbed anybody nor committed a murder." None of the two–three people who could have afforded to purchase the farm at its real value bid for it. However, we could not till that land either.'

Then, a maternal uncle gave them a pair of bullocks and a cart. 'So we could earn something by renting that out.'

'My grandmother would dig out something from the fields. My aunt and I would feed the bullocks. Our cart—and our lives—depended on them, so we had to take care of those animals properly.

'We would transport jaggery, groundnuts, jowar. If the cart went to Takari village, about twelve kilometres away, we earned three rupees. If it went all the way to Karad, over twenty kilometres away, then five rupees. That's all we earned.'

The family, however, never caved in to the torment of the Raj. By 1939, Hausabai would be an active member of the revolutionary underground, coordinating with her father and his comrades. The family continued to live in that one room till Independence in 1947. She vividly remembers the period from 1929 to 1946 as years of great suffering.

'And me? We would dig out grass from the fields—and how much could I have brought or carried? I was not yet 4 and my aunt was 9 when they seized our farm—how much could we young ones do? We couldn't work like the grownups. So we would labour a little bit and then rest a while in the shade.'

Hunger was a normal state of being.

'And my grandmother—her blouses were all torn. We had no money. So she took an old *lungi* of my father's and, cutting it in half, made two white blouses out of it. Later, when we had a little money, we got new ones for her, but she didn't touch them. All the way to Independence and the return of our family's properties, she wore those same two blouses made from her son's *lungi*.' Her own, very personal protest.

Even after Independence, says Hausatai, her grandmother Gojarabai Ramchandra Patil would not return to coloured blouses, sticking to white. 'Until she died, in 1963, she wore only those white blouses.'

This would be no midnight cruise on the Mandovi. Pleasures of that sort were as yet decades, perhaps an era, away. At that time of the night, there were more likely a couple of crocodiles, rather than boats and humans, cruising around the river.

Hausabai and her band of Toofan Sena comrades stood before the Mandovi where it made its way through a heavily forested area they'd been sticking to, as they sought to leave Portuguese-ruled Goa following a major escapade there. The crossing had to be done at night, to attract the least attention.

Their Goa mission, in 1944, was to free a comrade who had been arrested by the Portuguese police while transporting weapons from there to the Toofan Sena headquarters in Satara. It was not uncommon for Indian revolutionaries, particularly those in Maharashtra, to shop for firearms in Goa. Buying weapons there was easier than obtaining them back home. But transporting them out, under the eyes of another punitive colonial regime that was hardly encouraging of revolutionaries, was a different matter altogether.

In her Goa adventure, Hausatai was led and accompanied by the legendary G. D. Bapu Lad—a founder and leader of the Toofan Sena and a vital figure in the *prati sarkar*.

'So there was this worker, a Bal Joshi, who had been arrested while trying to bring back weapons from Goa. He could have been hanged. Bapu said, "We cannot return until we get him out of that jail."'

Hausabai managed to meet Joshi in the Panjim Central Jail, gaining access by posing as his sister, with an escape plan 'written on a small chit of paper that I hid in my hair bun'. However, they also had also to pick up weapons for the Toofan Sena, those that had not fallen into police hands. Now the return was even more risky.

'The policemen had all seen me and would recognize me.' So they chose road travel over the railways. Which essentially meant walking many miles through dense forests. 'But at the spot where we reached the Mandovi river, there was no boat, not even a small fishing boat. Then we knew we had to swim across. Or we might get arrested. But how would I go across? Suddenly, we found a big wooden box kept inside a fishing net.'

Lying on top the box, which served as a tiny and uncomfortable raft, she floated across the river at midnight, aided by her comrades swimming alongside, pushing or pulling the box.

'I could swim in a well or a tank,' says Hausatai, 'but this was flowing water. Too much for me. That Mandovi river is not a small one. I couldn't fall asleep on the box; we couldn't let it sink. Those Toofan Sena workers with us, they tied their dry clothes on top of their heads—to wear afterwards. I lay on my stomach upon the box.' And that strange crossing, surely a sight to behold were it not executed in total darkness, proceeded in silence.

'After crossing the river, we walked ahead through the forest, there was a path there. If we went on the main road, the police would arrest us—instead, we walked through the forest for two days. Somehow, we found our way out of the wilderness. It took us all of fifteen days to return home.'

The weapons the group had gone to pick up had escaped the police and were still with their contacts in Goa. But Hausabai and Bapu Lad did not retrieve these themselves. They knew that with Hausabai having visited the Panjim Central Jail, she might be easily recognized by Goa police on their homeward journey. So, they made other arrangements for the transportation of the weapons to Satara.

Some days later, Bal Joshi pulled off a successful jailbreak coordinated by his comrades outside the prison. The 'small chit of paper' Hausabai says she 'hid in my hair bun' had connected Joshi and his comrades.

Hausabai's job in the underground, prior to the spectacular events at the Bhavani Nagar police station and the Goa mission, was mainly intelligence gathering. With others, she picked up information for attacks like the one at Vangi (in present-day Satara district) in 1942, where a *dak* bungalow was set ablaze. 'The task of finding out how many policemen, when do they come and go, when would these places be least defended—this was their work,' says her son, Advocate Subhash Patil. 'Burning the bungalows was done by other squads.' There were many *dak* bungalows in that area. 'They burned them all.'

Since *dak* bungalows were important to the administrative machinery, this act disrupted the routine functioning of the Raj in Satara. Hausabai and her squad also picked up details on the transportation of postal bags—by train, only occasionally by bus. This advance information enabled the Toofan Sena's boarding, halting and looting of those bags from trains and buses.

We are nearing the end of our interview with Hausabai in Vita. She is intrigued by the concept of the People's Archive of Rural India (PARI) and happy that we are interested in documenting and recording the lives of India's last living freedom fighters, like herself, in their own words.

In 1972, with India completing twenty-five years of Independence, an initiative was undertaken to recognize freedom fighters. But people like Hausabai, who escaped jail or imprisonment, lacked the 'proof' required for formal recognition. Official recognition did come later, though—in 1992.

Pic: Namita Waikar/PARI

Hausabai with her family in Vita town in Sangli, Maharashtra in 2017.

She herself has not run after any certification from the state. Yet, the importance PARI gives freedom fighters like her pleased Hausabai.

Were there other women in the underground like her? Yes, she says, rattling off names without hesitation. 'Shalutai, the teacher's wife, Lilatai Patil, Lakshmibai Naikvadi, Rajmati Patil—those were some of the women.'

Many of Hausabai 's adventures were in the company of 'Shelar Mama' and the revolutionary G. D. Bapu Lad. 'Shelar Mama' was the nickname of her comrade Krishna Salunkhe. (The original Shelar Mama was a famous seventeenth-century Maratha warrior.)

Bapu Lad was there in all her major missions. He would pose as 'as my cousin, my mother's sister's son', she says. This was necessary because 'people don't lose a chance to raise suspicions. But my husband Bhagwanrao Nanasaheb More Patil [the Toofan

Sena's Khanapur unit chief] knew that Bapu and I were truly like brother and sister. There was a warrant out in my husband's name as well. When we went to Goa, it was only me and Bapu and the Toofan Sena team together. At other times, Bapu would always send me messages—"Don't sit at home! Be active."'

Hausabai played the role of Bapu Lad's mother's sister's daughter so often that even today she lapses into calling him her cousin. With Shelar Mama, she pretended they were father and daughter. The true-life dramas they enacted were many, their risks very real—and the results a constant harassment of the colonial Raj. Yet, she insists again, 'I did some little work in the freedom struggle. I did not do anything great.'

Hausabai is unhappy with the present situation in the country. She feels farmers are being treated badly. And worries about people caving in to pressure. 'Nowadays, if one person is arrested, the others don't go forward. The problems will be solved, but it will take time. There are some good people also, and things will get better, but it will take time.'

As we wind up the interview and start packing, Hausabai has one more surprise for us. Her eyes gleaming, she asks: 'So, are you going to take me now?'

'But where to, Hausabai?'

'To work with you all at PARI,' she says laughing.

'I appeal to the government not to sleep . . .'

That was the inimitable Hausabai Patil, in a video message to the giant farmers' march on Parliament in November 2018.

Hauling up the government, but also telling the farmers they had to fight for their rights. She had always held that mass struggles and public action was the way forward—'it will take time, but things will get better'.

'Farmers must get better prices for their crops,' she thundered. 'To get this justice, I'll come there myself' and join the march, she told the protestors in the video. Never mind that she was already nearly 93 and not in the best of health. She called on the government 'not to sleep but to wake up and work for the poor'.

On 23 September 2021, the ever-awake and alert Hausabai entered her own final sleep in Sangli at age 95.

Like many of her contemporaries, Hausabai fought for both freedom and independence. Hers was a patriotism driven by the need to unite and liberate Indians from British imperialism, not divide them on grounds of religion or caste. A secular spirit entwined with the ideologies of hope and not hatred.

A foot soldier of freedom, not of fanaticism.

Scan QR code for PARI Freedom Fighters Gallery.

2

WHEN DEMATI DEI 'SALIHAN' TOOK ON THE RAJ

'They destroyed our homes, our crops. And they attacked my father. Of course, I had to fight them.'

—Demati Dei Sabar 'Salihan', Purena village,
Bargarh, Odisha

She was working in the forests and fields with others when a youngster from their village came racing towards them, yelling, 'They're attacking us, they have assaulted your father. They are torching our homes.'

'They' were armed British police, cracking down on a rebellious region seen as defiant of the Raj. 'She' whose father had been wounded was Demati Dei Sabar, then barely 16. Many other villages besides her own, Saliha, had been attacked.

15

Some were completely burned down and their grain looted. The rebels were being shown their place.

Demati, an Adivasi of the Sabar tribe, raced back to Saliha with forty other young women. 'My father lay bleeding on the ground,' the ageing freedom fighter tells us. 'He had a bullet in his leg.'

That memory brings alive a mind otherwise fading. 'I lost my temper and attacked the officer who had a gun. In those days, we all took lathis as we went to work in the forest or fields. You had to have something with you in case wild animals showed up.' And they often did—wild boar, wolves, aggressive monkeys, even big cats. Which meant carrying your lathi was not enough. You needed to know how to use it.

Demati, as the officer discovered, did.

As she attacked him, the forty other women with her turned their lathis on the rest of the raiding force. 'I chased the scoundrel down the street,' she says, angry, but also chuckling, 'raining blows on him.' He was too surprised to do anything else. He ran, he ran.' She beat and chased the man around the village. She then picked up her father and took him away from the spot. He was arrested a little later, though. Kartik Sabar was a key organizer of anti-British meetings in the area.

Demati Dei Sabar is known as 'Salihan' after the village Saliha, also called Salihagarh, in Nuapada, where she was born. Nuapada was carved out of the Kalahandi region as a separate district in 1993. Demati was a freedom fighter of Odisha who had taken on a gun-toting British police squad with a lathi.

There is a fearlessness about her, still. She does not believe that she did anything extraordinary. Well, she doesn't dwell on it anyway. 'They destroyed our homes, our crops. And they attacked my father. Of course, I had to fight them.'

The year was 1930. The Raj was cracking down on pro-Independence meetings being held in the rebellious region. Demati's charge against the British and their police was the most dramatic point of what came to be known as the Saliha Uprising and firing.

Demati is still alive, closing in on 90, when I meet her in 2002. There is still strength and beauty in her face. Emaciated and fast losing her sight now, but probably very beautiful, tall and strong when young. Her long arms, which still hint at hidden vigour, must have wielded a mean lathi. That officer must have had a rough time. He certainly had the right idea in running.

Her incredible courage went unrewarded and, outside her village, is largely forgotten.

'Salihan' lives in degrading poverty in Purena village of Bargarh district. A multi-coloured official certificate authenticating her heroism is her most prized possession. That too, speaks more of her father than of her and does not record the counterattack she led. She has no pension, no assistance from the state at the time we meet her.

She is losing her memory and peers at us, somewhat uncomprehending, as we shoot questions at her.

And then comes the query that brings it all back.

'You must have been angry and upset when you saw your father lying in the street, bleeding from his bullet wound?'

With that, the almost-nonagenarian comes alive. With an anger that relit the past as present. Her voice quivering with a wrath that has not abated in decades. Like it is all happening right now, right in front of her. It also rekindles other memories.

Demati Dei Sabar 'Salihan' at her home in Purena village Bargarh, Odisha, when we met her in 2002.

'My elder sister Bhan Dei, and Gangatelen and Sakhatoren [two other women of Saliha village]—they too were arrested. They're all gone now. Father spent two years in Raipur Jail.' And several months in Nagpur prison as well, but she does not recall that.

What she does recall is going after that officer—recorded history does not give us his name. She is quite modest and shy about how her bold charge inspired the other women, indeed the entire village, to regroup and strike back, driving the British force out of Saliha.

Her region today is dominated by feudal elements who were collaborators of the Raj. They have benefited more from the freedom that Salihan and her kind fought for. Islands of wealth dot the ocean of deprivation here. She gives us a great smile, many great smiles, but she is tiring. She struggles to recall the names of her three sons—Bishnu, Akura and Sakura Bhoi. Likewise with the names of her daughters—Ukia, Maharagi and Janaki Bhoi.

Apparently, she remembers them well when she sees them. Those of them still alive. What she never forgets is the Saliha Uprising. And her role in it.

She clutches at the once-colourful, now decaying piece of paper that a family member produces at her command. Salihan hands it to us to read, without a word. For Salihan herself can neither read nor write.

The Sabar people have endured a long history of oppression and discrimination. And their literacy, numeracy and presence in schools remain poor even today. That ill-treatment, historically, was not confined to the economic sphere. The deity we now know as Lord Jagannath actually had humble tribal origins with the Savar or Sabar people who worshipped him as 'Neela Madhaba'.

'The deity was appropriated centuries ago by powerful upper castes,' says Fanindam Deo, historian and former principal of the Khariar Autonomous College in Nuapada district. And by the nineteenth century, he says, the Sabar found themselves barred from entry to the Jagannath temple at Puri. Lord Jagannath was by then 'in the grip of a *raja–brahmana* [royal elite–Brahmin] nexus.' A list issued by the Brahmins controlling the temple had banned the entry of 'bird eaters' on its premises. The forest-dwelling Sabars, points out Professor Deo, obviously fell into that category.

This is a tribe living with that historic loss of their god and subsequent decline in status over a thousand years. As the British appropriated the great timber wealth of Odisha, tribes like the Sabar—who relied on the forests and did very little agriculture—saw their world crumble. They and other Adivasi groups were terrorized and increasingly denied access to their own forests.

In 1929 and 1930, the cruel imposition of a timber or 'wood' tax harassed the forest dwellers further. Together with the *gochar* or grazing tax, says historian Jitamitra Prasad Singh Deo in Khariar, this was to prove both a major source of discontent, and of mass mobilization, for the Civil Disobedience stir and the Salt Satyagraha in this area. Which increasingly took the shape of a 'jungle satyagraha' in a landlocked region without salt. 'National political cyclones,' he says, 'saw winds of unrest sweep Odisha as well.'

There was also the *pandhri* or *pandhari* tax—an entry tax (something like octroi) levied on anyone coming into the Khariar *zamindari*. This, along with the *abkari* (excise), forest and police administration, had been taken over by the British in the 1890s.

It was in this larger context of ferment and turmoil that not just Saliha but several other villages in the Nuapada–Khariar region erupted, says Singh Deo (who is also the former ruler of the erstwhile Khariar zamindari). And the timber and *gochar* taxes were crucial issues in a protest meeting held in Saliha and attended by people from other villages as well. There, says Singh Deo, a resolution was passed not to pay the taxes and to resist their imposition. That fateful meeting was held in Saliha on 30 September 1930, the day of the attack on that village by the British.

That was also the day Demati Dei Salihan entered the hearts of her people, but never their history books.

Over six decades after her fearless fight-back against the British, Salihan was presented—by a rather low-level functionary of the Odisha government—with a *maana patra* (certificate of honour). My old friend and fellow journalist Purusottam Thakur takes it from her and translates it for me on the spot—and it is unjust and appalling.

The certificate for Salihan is really a eulogy for her father. Her role, as understood by the certificate's authors, is mentioned in a few lines—implying that her bravery arose from being her father's daughter. And that her achievement was picking up her wounded parent from the street where he lay and taking him back to safety. Not a word about the British force being counterattacked and beaten back by villagers— mainly women—inspired by her death-defying charge.

The other mention of her is that she 'bears three sons'. She also has three daughters, but that was not found worthy of mention.

21

Certificate of Honour
(*maana patra*)

Amar Senani (Martyr): Kartik Sabar
Village: Saliha
District: Nuapada

O Kranti Veer!

Today, on this auspicious occasion we are proud of your significant role in the freedom movement of India.

Despite being born in a remote and unknown village called 'Saliha', you were inspired by the call of Mahatma Gandhi and entered into the freedom struggle and left a record of glorious contribution.

You faced the wrath of the British Government by leading and organizing a public meeting at Saliha. The force resorted to lathi charge and firing in order to wreak havoc on the public gathering. You [Kartik Sabar] were cruelly beaten and fell injured and bleeding on the mother earth.

Following your footsteps, your sixteen-year-old daughter Demati Dei reached the meeting venue with a number of women followers. At that time, they saw you completely blood stained.

But the brilliant flare of Independence was emanating from her. She did not turn away and instead carried you back to the village.

When you became conscious and recovered you once again led the movement, whereupon you were arrested and put behind bars for two years at Raipur Jail.

Today we gratefully honour your great sacrifice by felicitating your capable daughter.

That your immortal soul inspires us to act to for the protection of Independence—that is our sincere prayer.

About Demati Dei

She bears three sons. They are Bishnu Bhoi, Akura Bhoi and Sakura Bhoi.

Millions of poor Indian women—so many Salihans—fought for this nation's freedom as bravely as anyone else. Only very few, like Salihan herself, achieved even the status of a fading footnote in the history of that struggle. But the only anger in her is still directed at the British police she fought. Barring when she recalls her father's lying bleeding in the street, she has been smiling at us throughout. Even while showing us the ridiculous certificate of honour.

She waves at us as we say goodbye and leave. Demati Dei 'Salihan' is still smiling.

23

In Purena Village, Bargarh, Twenty Years After

'We don't have that certificate of honour anymore,' says Hemanta Bhoi, Salihan's grandson. 'Nor any other document of our grandmother. Not even a photograph. Two journalists came here and took it all away, promising to return it to us after some verification. But they never did.'

Their names? 'All we know is that one was from Khariar and the other from Komna. That's what they told us,' says Jasabanta Bhoi, another grandson of Salihan.

Purusottam Thakur and I (for we are together again at her home after twenty years) begin to figure out that this has something to do with us. After my first visit to Purena and Saliha (which I also spoke about across Odisha)—officials, even Ministers, had landed up at both villages. And in their wake, some journalists.

We're meeting twelve relatives of Salihan in their little, dilapidated corner of Purena. Three grandsons, their wives, some great-grandchildren. Their condition is not much better than what we found Salihan living in when she was alive, twenty years ago.

As always, the Adivasis, who were the first to die for freedom, are the last to benefit from it. The family is absorbing, once again, the realization that they will never see the only possessions connecting them to the memory of their most illustrious member. Unless, of course, the journalists have cared to retain the papers after they got 'their story'. Which seems unlikely after twenty years.

The descendants of Salihan, including her grandsons, their wives and children in Purena, Odisha in 2022.

This does happen sometimes, when a few journalists from the towns, typically of a higher class and caste, deal with poor and marginalized people they don't really care about. I saw it happen while covering farmers' suicides in different states. A journalist descending from a big town or city—sometimes television reporters seeking 'visuals' of documents—pick up the family's only photos and albums assuring them their precious possessions would be returned. Some do honour that assurance. A few don't.

It also happens that this is sometimes done in a competitive spirit—to deny the next reporter arriving there a visual. And yes, sometimes a small sum of money too is taken from the suicide-hit family, with the promise of running an obituary in whichever newspaper grabbed those pics 'exclusively'.

'They said the Collector had sent them to take the documents back to the district headquarters for verification,' says Kulamani Bhoi, also a grandson. Hemanta and Jasabanta are in their late forties, Kulamani in his late fifties. All are marginal cultivators who pick up any other work they can to feed their families.

Pic: P. Sainath/PARI

Kulamani Bhoi, a grandson of Salihan in Purena,
enacts the drama of how she wielded the lathi in
fighting the British police.

'I am still proud of her,' says Phagulal Bhoi, a great-grandson. He is 24 and would have been barely 3 when she died. That is, a little over a year, after our meeting with her in 2002. He is a migrant worker, presently on duty as a security guard at one of the Accenture offices in Bengaluru. But that is a contract appointment with a security services company to whom corporations outsource such work. He has no certainty of tenure. And he went through a troubled time in the first nationwide lockdown that began at midnight of 24–25 March 2020. None of Salihan's descendants holds a steady job. All live in poverty as she did.

All of them, like Phagulal, take pride in Salihan's bravery. And tell us she too was actually quite proud of her courageous counterattack. 'She spoke to us of taxes and torture under the British *sarkar*,' says Jasabanta. And Kulamani, the oldest of the group, gives us a physical enactment of her gripping the lathi and wading into the police. There is pride on every one of the twelve faces, including his own, as he does this.

Somebody, after all, still remembers Salihan.

In Saliha, a monument—costing lakhs of rupees so far and likely to run to crores—records the names of seventeen people arrested, including one who died soon after of his wounds, in the uprising of 30 September 1930. Certainly, people worthy of remembrance. The official district website even carries a photograph of the memorial pillar here and promotes the village as a tourism spot on that count.

But there are two names that are missing from the commemorative pillar: Demati Dei Sabar 'Salihan' and her father Kartik Sabar.

It could be argued that Salihan herself was not arrested at that time—but her wounded and bloodied father certainly was. Kartik was held soon after and thrown into Raipur Jail for two years. He also spent some months in Nagpur prison. Khariar of that time came under the Central Provinces.

But no one is making such an argument—the officials of the 'Salihagarh Shaheed Smriti Parishad' in fact make a different and more astonishing claim: 'Of course both their names are there,' says 60-year-old Mahesh Ram Sahu, President of the committee and a shopkeeper and trader in the village, at his residence. The committee raises funds, much of it from the government, and oversees the ongoing construction of the complex where the pillar-monument is located.

Sahu whips out a photocopied pamphlet with a list and says: 'See? Both names are there on our list.'

We point out to him that we met him a couple of hours earlier at the monument and had photographed him there standing beside it. And show him the close-up photographs of the pillar and the inscription on it. No Salihan, no Kartik Sabar.

'I do not know how this could have happened,' he says, seemingly surprised. 'We shall of course correct it.' I think of others who have made the Sabars promises, including the two reporters who said they would return Salihan's records to her family. We're not certain, but it does appear there are no Sabars on the memorial committee.

The Sabars themselves are startled. 'But surely their names are there,' says Menghraj Sabar, who is kin to the family of Kartik Sabar. Menghraj has been taking us around the village and its surrounding forests.

'We were promised their names would be there. We were told they *are* there,' protests Menghraj. Did he check it out? Not really—the Sabars of Salihagarh are still largely illiterate.

There are even those who argue that we cannot really call the Salihans of the era freedom fighters. She was not a part of the Independence struggle nor of a political movement, they argue. She had not gone to jail. But neither did some of India's great underground revolutionaries.

I also remember the question Laxmi Panda (see Chapter 9)—the Odia woman who joined Netaji Bose's Indian National Army—once asked me: 'Because I killed no one, because I did not go to jail—we were underground workers in forest camps—am I not a freedom fighter? Did I not resist the British? Did I make no contribution to the struggle?'

Salihan resisted the British with an energy and spirit hard to rival. She fought in defence of her family and village against an armed attack by a colonial power. She was one among many in the region challenging British imperialism, its laws, its rules and its Raj. Her battle was for rights craved by millions of others. No one can ever take away what she was: a fighter for freedom.

We are now looking for Ganpat Sabar and Bhanatram Sabar, both great-nephews of Salihan. But Bhanatram, who knows a lot, vanishes into the forests. He does that the moment he spots us.

With the help of his brother and Menghraj, we track him down in the forests and persuade him to talk to us. And he has much to say of his illustrious relative. All three are astonished to learn that Salihan and Kartik do not appear on the list of names on the pillar in their own village. They are proud of Salihan and of the role of tribals in the 1930 uprising.

Even today, ninety years after the revolt, fully a third of Saliha's people are Adivasis. In 1930, when this village was in the midst of far denser forest, they accounted for most of those who lived here. Besides that, tribals led the uprising of that year. Yet, there are just two Adivasis' names on the pillar, which confuses and hurts Bhanatram, Ganpat and Menghraj.

And no mention of Salihan and Kartik. The whole thing puzzles Professor Fanindam Deo. As part of a team from Khariar College, he was present when the pillar was unveiled. That was on 10 September 1997, marking the sixty-seventh anniversary of the Saliha revolt. And as part of the fifty-year celebrations of Indian Independence. 'There were no names on the monument at all,' says Professor Deo. 'And Salihan was alive and present at the function. As a special invitee.'

That was when she received her not-so-special *maana patra*. 'The seventeen names were probably added around 2008,' he says.

Both Salihan and Kartik were dead by then. Now they have been, in a further sense, 'disappeared'.

But back to Bhanatram, who is now speaking freely.

Why, we ask him, did you run off on seeing us?

'Well, you came in an SUV,' he explains. 'Obviously, I thought you were from the Forest Department. They are always harassing us Sabars.'

Like they did over 130 years ago during the British Raj. Like they did in the run-up to the uprising that Salihan led.

Like they still do, today.

A personal postscript: It was in 2002, the Gujarat riots had happened, new temples were coming up in and around Saliha, that we met Demati Dei on our first trip to Purena. And also to her village of origin. There were four of us apart from the driver, and we were in the vehicle, leaving after our meeting with her.

Normally a noisy, raucous gang, we were all completely silent, some of us close to tears. We had interacted with selflessness and sacrifice, with goodness and grace, but were mostly overwhelmed by the sheer injustice endured by a woman who fought for freedom and asked for nothing in return for herself. Who said not a word about that personal injustice in her meeting with us. We in the vehicle were numb and silent. I wondered how I was going to write about it.

I could not write a piece on her for quite some time. As we drove away, I scribbled the only thing I could at that moment, in the car—a few verses for Demati Dei Sabar Salihan. (If interested in those personal scribbles, see Annexure 1.)

Scan QR code for PARI Freedom Fighters Gallery.

3

BHAGAT SINGH JHUGGIAN'S FIGHT FOR OUR FREEDOMS

'There were two sets of people here in August 1947. One set killing Muslims, another trying to save them from the attackers.'

—Bhagat Singh Jhuggian, Fighter with the revolutionary underground, Ramgarh village, Hoshiarpur, Punjab

He was on stage to receive his prize—a shiny one-paisa coin—from the Munshi, a senior officer with several schools under his control. This was Punjab in 1939; he was just 11 years old and a student of Class III, which he had just topped. The Munshi patted him on the head and asked him to shout 'Britannia Zindabad, Hitler Murdabad'. Young Bhagat

Singh—not to be confused with his legendary namesake—faced the audience at the ceremony and yelled: 'Britannia Murdabad, Hindustan Zindabad.'

The consequences of his impudence were immediate. He was thrashed then and there by the Munshi himself, wielding a *tooth di chhadi*. That's a stick of mulberry wood—a harsh weapon of punishment in rural Punjab. He was also thrown out of the Government Elementary School, Samundra.

The other students present stared in shocked silence, and then ran away. The local schools' authority—someone we might today call the district education officer—issued a letter with the assent of the deputy commissioner in this part of what is now the Hoshiarpur district in Punjab.

The letter confirmed Bhagat Singh's expulsion, describing him as 'dangerous' and a 'revolutionary'—at age 11!

This simply meant no school—and there weren't too many around—would ever let the blacklisted Bhagat Singh Jhuggian enter their gates. Many besides his parents begged the authorities to reverse their decision. One well-connected *zaildar* (major landlord), Ghulam Mustafa, from the nearby village of Saroya, made strenuous efforts on his behalf. But the minions of the Raj were furious. A little boy had shamed their dignitary. Bhagat Singh Jhuggian never returned to formal education for the rest of his extraordinarily colourful and ongoing life.

But he was and remains, at age 93, a star pupil of the school of hard knocks. He smiles at the recollection of the drama, speaking to us at his home in Ramgarh village of Hoshiarpur district. Didn't he feel awful about it? Well, he says, 'My reaction was—now I am free to join the anti-British struggle.'

That he was free to do so had not gone unnoticed. Though at first he went and worked on his family's five-acre farm, his fame spread. Groups from Punjab's radical underground began to contact him. 'They were from the Kirti Party, and included Kalyan Singh Dhillon, Baba Bhagwan Das and others.'

He joined the Kirti Party, an offshoot of the Ghadar Party that had staged the Ghadar revolt of 1914–15 in the state.

The Kirti Party comprised many who had gone to revolutionary Russia for military and ideological training. On returning to a Punjab where the Ghadar movement had been crushed, they started a publication called *Kirti*. Among its most distinguished journalist contributors was the other, legendary Bhagat Singh, who in fact ran *Kirti* for three months before his arrest on 27 May 1927. In May 1942, the Kirti Party merged with the Communist Party of India.

And no, Jhuggian was not named after the great Bhagat Singh, though, he says, 'I grew up hearing people sing songs of him—there were many.' He even recites a few words of one from that period on the great revolutionary who was hanged by the British in 1931, when his tiny namesake was just 3 years old. '*Bhagat Singh Hun Lagnge Tere Mele*' ('Bhagat Singh! Now you will be celebrated in festivals!').

In the years after his expulsion from school, the young Bhagat Singh Jhuggian became a courier for the revolutionary underground. Between working on his family's farmland, 'I would do anything they asked me to do'. One of those things, while still a teenager, was walking over twenty kilometres in darkness, carrying a small, dismantled and 'horribly heavy' printing press in two sacks to a secret camp of the revolutionaries. Literally, a foot soldier of freedom.

'At the other end also they gave me a heavy bag of food and other supplies to carry across the same distance to comrades in our network.' His family also provided food and shelter to underground fighters.

The machine he transported was called an '*udaaru* press' (literally, 'flying press', but meaning a portable one). It is not clear whether it was a dismantled press, or vital parts of one, or a cyclostyling machine. He just remembers that 'it had large and heavy cast iron parts'. Old-timers in their eighties say that such a description suggests it would have been a dismantled small printing press.

He came through his courier era mostly unscathed, never saying no to risk and danger—and proud that over the years, the 'police were more scared of me than I was of them'.

And then Partition happened.

It's when talking about that period that Bhagat Singh Jhuggian gets most emotional. The old gentleman fights his tears as he speaks of the mayhem and mass murder of the time. 'The caravan of people in countless thousands leaving to cross the border was frequently attacked, people slaughtered. There were massacres right around here.'

'It was in Simbli village just four kilometres away,' says schoolteacher, writer and local historian Ajmer Sidhu, 'that about 250 people, all of them Muslims, were butchered in two nights and one day.' Yet, says Sidhu, who is with us when we interview Bhagat Singh Jhuggian, 'Of these, the *thanadar* of the Garhshankar police station recorded only 101 deaths.'

'There were two sets of people here in August 1947. One set killing Muslims, another trying to save them from the attackers,' says Bhagat Singh.

'A young man was shot dead near my field. We offered to help his brother cremate him, but he was terrified and went ahead with the caravan. We buried the body in our own field. It was not a nice 15 August here,' he adds.

Among those who managed to cross the border was Ghulam Mustafa, the landowner who had once tried to get Bhagat Singh Jhuggian back in school.

'However,' says Bhagat Singh, 'Mustafa's son, Abdul Rahman, had stayed on a little longer and was in grave danger. My family brought Rahman stealthily to our house one night. He had a horse with him.'

But the mobs out hunting for Muslims got wind of this. 'So one night we smuggled him out, and through a network of friends and comrades, he managed to cross the border in one piece.' Later, they even returned the horse to him across the border. Mustafa, in letters to friends in the village, thanked Jhuggian and promised to visit him in India one day. 'But he never came back.'

Talking of the Partition makes Bhagat Singh sad and uncomfortable. He is silent for a few moments before speaking again. He was jailed briefly, for seventeen days, when the police broke up a conference on the freedom struggle in Birampur village, also in Hoshiarpur.

In 1948, he joined the Lal (Red) Communist Party Hind Union, a breakaway group from the erstwhile Kirti Party that had merged with the CPI.

But that was the time all Communist groups were banned, between 1948 and 1951, following the uprisings in Telangana and elsewhere. Bhagat Singh Jhuggian returned to his role of farmer by day, secret courier by night. And host to underground activists on the run. He himself spent a year underground in this phase of his life.

Later, in 1952, the Lal Party merged with the Communist Party of India. When the CPI split in 1964, he threw in his lot with the newly formed CPI-M, with which he would remain.

Through that period, he participated in land and other struggles affecting farmers. Bhagat Singh was arrested in 1959 during the *Khush Hasiyati* tax morcha (anti-betterment tax struggle). His crime: mobilizing farmers of the Kandi area (now in Punjab's northeastern border). A furious Partap Singh Kairon government punished him by seizing his buffalo and fodder-chopping machine and auctioning them. But both were purchased for eleven rupees by a fellow villager, who then returned them to the family.

Bhagat Singh also spent three months in Ludhiana Jail during this agitation. And again, three months in Patiala Jail later the same year.

The village where he has lived all his life was at first a collection of *jhuggis* (slum dwellings) and came to be called Jhuggian. Hence the name Bhagat Singh Jhuggian. It is now part of Ramgarh village in Garhshankar tehsil.

In 1975, he again went underground for a year, fighting the Emergency—mobilizing people, playing courier when he had to, distributing anti-Emergency literature.

Through all these years, he remained rooted in his village and region. The man who had never made it past Class III took a deep interest in youngsters around him struggling with education and employment. Many of those he helped would do well, some even making it to government service.

Pic: Courtesy of family of Bhagat Singh Jhuggian

A young Bhagat Singh with wife and child. The photo is perhaps from the 1960s.

Bhagat Singh Jhuggian sometime in the late 1970s or in the 1980s.

1990: Bhagat Singh's family was aware there were only minutes between them, their tube well and terror. The heavily armed Khalistani hit squad had paused in their fields, confirming their target from his name inscribed on the tube well barely four hundred metres from their home. There they lay in ambush, but had been seen.

From 1984 to 1993, Punjab was tormented by terror. Hundreds of people were gunned down, assassinated or otherwise murdered. Among them large numbers of activists from the CPI, the CPI-M and CPI-ML, as those parties offered stubborn resistance to the Khalistanis. Bhagat Singh was always on the hit list in this period.

It was in 1990, though, that he came closest to finding out what it meant to be on that list. His three young sons were on the roof, with guns given to them by the police. It was a time when the government allowed, even assisted, people under death threat to arm themselves for self-defence.

'What they [the government] gave us, those guns were not very good ones. So I borrowed a 12-bore shotgun and even bought a second-hand one myself later,' says Bhagat Singh, recalling the period.

His son Paramjit, 50, says, 'Once, I opened and read a threat letter to my father from the terrorists: "Stop your activities or your entire family will be wiped out." I put it back in the cover and pretended nobody had seen it. I wondered how my father would react. He calmly read the letter, folded it and placed it in his pocket. Moments later, he took the three of us to the roof and asked us to be alert. But didn't say a word about the letter.'

The 1990 stand-off was spine-chilling. There was no doubt this gutsy family would fight to the last. But in all probability, they would have been overwhelmed by the firepower of the trained hit squad armed with AK-47s and other deadly weapons.

That was when one of the extremists recognized the name on the tube well. 'He turned to the others and said, "If it is Bhagat Singh Jhuggian who is our target, I will have nothing to do with this,"' says the old freedom fighter. The hit squad decided to call off its mission, and withdrew from the field and vanished.

It turned out the militant's younger brother was one of those youths Bhagat Singh had helped. Who had in fact gone on to get a government job—as a *patwari* (keeper of village records). 'For two years after they withdrew,' says Bhagat Singh smiling, 'that older brother would send me tip-offs and warnings. When and where not to go . . .' This helped him evade further attempts on his life.

The manner in which the family speaks of the episode is almost unsettling. Bhagat Singh's analysis of it is clinical. He is far more emotional when speaking of Partition. What about his wife, was she not shaken at the time? 'I was confident we could counter the attack,' says Gurdev Kaur, 78, most calmly. A veteran activist of the All-India Democratic Women's Association, she says, 'My sons were strong, I had no fear—and the village supported us.'

Gurdev Kaur married Bhagat Singh in 1961—his second marriage. His first wife died a few years after their wedding in 1944, and the two daughters they had have settled abroad. Gurdev Kaur and he had three sons from their marriage, but the eldest, Jasveer Singh, died in 2011 aged 47. The two others are Kuldeep Singh, 55, now in the United Kingdom, and Paramjit, who lives with them.

Does he still have the 12-bore gun? 'No, I got rid of it. Of what use would it be now—a child could snatch it from my hands,' laughs the 93-year-old. I look at his wiry, gnarled fingers and figure a strong adult might find that difficult.

The 1992 state Assembly elections brought danger back to his doorstep. The central government was determined to hold elections in Punjab. The Khalistanis, equally set on paralysing the polls, started killing candidates.[*] Under Section 52 of the Representation of the People Act of 1951, the death of a candidate of a recognized political party during the campaign leads to 'adjournment' or countermanding of the election in that constituency.

Every candidate was now at grave risk.

Indeed, unparalleled levels of violence had led to the postponement of these very polls in June 1991. Between March and June that year, as a paper by Gurharpal Singh in the journal *Asian Survey* points out, '24 state and parliamentary candidates were killed; 76 passengers on two trains were massacred; and a week before polling, Punjab was declared a disturbed area.'

---

[*] 'The Punjab Elections 1992: Breakthrough or Breakdown?', Gurharpal Singh, *Asian Survey*, Vol. 32, No. 11, November 1992

Pic: Courtesy of family of Bhagat Singh Jhuggian

Bhagat Singh Jhuggian campaigning as a candidate in the 1992
Punjab elections while on the hit list of Khalistani terrorists.

So the aim of the extremists was clear. Kill enough candidates.
The government responded by providing unprecedented
levels of security to candidates. Among them, Bhagat Singh
Jhuggian, who contested the polls from the Garhshankar
constituency. All factions of the Akali Dal boycotted the polls.
'Every candidate,' as Gurharpal Singh's paper notes, 'was
provided with a 32-person security detachment, and for more
prominent leaders the figure was 50 or higher.' Of course, all
this was only for the duration of the polls.

What of Bhagat Singh's contingent of thirty-two? 'There
were,' he says, 'eighteen security guards at my party office here.
Another twelve were with me always and would go wherever
I went on campaign. And two were always at home with my
family.' Having been on the terrorist hit list for years before
the election, his risks were greater. But he came through all

right. A massive security operation of the army, paramilitary and police personnel also countered the extremists—the polls were held without great casualties.

'He contested the 1992 election,' explains Paramjit, 'believing that by making himself a higher priority target, he would be saving his younger comrades by deflecting the attention of the Khalistanis in his own direction.'

Bhagat Singh lost the election to the Congress candidate. But he had been in others that he had won. In 1957, he was elected sarpanch of two villages, Ramgarh and Chak Gujjran. He was to be a sarpanch four times, his last stint being in 1998.

He was elected a director of the cooperative sugar mill in Nawanshahr (now Shaheed Bhagat Singh Nagar) in 1978. That was by defeating Sansar Singh, a powerful landlord allied with the Akali Dal. In 1998, he was again elected to the post—unanimously.

His mind keeps returning to the pogroms of Partition. Many people Bhagat Singh knew in his neighbourhood were among its victims. Including Afzal Tauseef of Simbli village, the girl he had narrowly beaten to become the class topper at school. As many as eighteen members of Tauseef's family were slaughtered. She moved to Lahore in 1947.

'I was ahead of Tauseef by a single mark,' says a deeply saddened Bhagat Singh. 'I was brought to Garhshankar for the function, where the Munshi *babuji* gave me that one paisa as a reward for being the topper in my class.' Not to forget, that brutal thrashing.

Tauseef went on to become one of Pakistan's most admired authors in the Punjabi language (written in the Shahmukhi script in Pakistan). She wrote in many newspapers and published close to thirty books on politics and contemporary issues. Tauseef retired as an English teacher at the College of Education, Lahore.

Bhagat Singh, the class topper, never spent another day in school.

Both, though, had political commitment and resolve. Tauseef was detained, even displaced several times by successive military dictatorships in Pakistan, whom she criticized. Bhagat Singh took on powerful feudals in land struggles. And went on to confront Khalistani terror as well.

Among Afzal Tauseef's better known books are: *Dekhi Teri Duniya* (I Have Seen Your World). And *Aman Vele Milange* (We Will Meet in the Time of Peace).

And she did return to India in a time of peace. A friend of writer and poet Amrita Pritam, Afzal Tauseef visited post-Partition India five times. She was not keen to return to Simbli. She found the memories it held too overwhelming for her. Yet, she did go there three times, persuaded by schoolteacher and local historian Ajmer Sidhu, who organized those visits.

Sadly, Afzal Tauseef, who died in 2014, never got to meet her Class III schoolmate Bhagat Singh Jhuggian on any of those trips to India.

Across those eight decades since he was thrashed and thrown out of school, Bhagat Singh Jhuggian has been and remains politically aware, alert and active. At our first and main meeting with him in August 2021, he wants to know everything that is happening in the ongoing farmers' protests. He sits on his party's State Control Commission. And is also a trustee of the body that runs the Desh Bhagat Yadgar Hall (DBYH) in Jalandhar. More than any other institution, the DBYH records, documents and memorializes the revolutionary movements of the Punjab. The trust itself was founded by revolutionaries of the Ghadar movement.

'Even today, when *jathas* [organized convoys of marchers] go out on farmers issues from this area, maybe to join the protest camps on Delhi's borders, they go first to comrade Bhagat Singh's house for his blessings,' says his friend Darshan Singh Mattu. A member of the CPI-M's Punjab State Committee, Mattu notes, 'He is physically restricted compared to earlier. But his commitment and intensity remain as strong as ever. Even now he is part of the effort in Ramgarh and Garhshankar to mobilize rice, oil, dal, other items and money, including his own personal contributions—for the protesting farmers camped at Shahjahanpur.'

I met Bhagat Singh Jhuggian again on 1 November 2021, this time during the thirtieth *'Mela Gadri Babeyan Da'* in the grounds of the Desh Bhagat Yadgar Hall complex. It's a three-day festival held annually to celebrate the memory of martyrs of the Ghadar rebellion and their dreams of freedom and a better world. The *mela* typically ends on the evening of 1 November with revolutionary ballads and plays.

This edition of the festival was dedicated to the farmers' protests, still on at the gates of Delhi on that day.

Bhagat Singh Jhuggian was there to hoist the Ghadar flag, getting on to the stage in a wheelchair. He had come down from his village in Hoshiarpur for the occasion. 'The efforts of our freedom fighters who fought for prosperity and social and economic equality must not go in vain,' he told an audience of over 3,000 that had gathered from all over Punjab. (Many times that number were watching the event live on the net around the world.)

Recognizing me from my visit to his home, he gave me a warm hug and then gripped my hands firmly and shook them. No, I thought, no child, or even adult, is going to grab a gun or anything from those hands.

He was very happy with the shorter version of his story that we carried in thirteen languages on the People's Archive of Rural India. When will the book come, he wanted to know? I promised him that around 15 August 2022, I would deliver a copy to him at his home.

On 13 March, in the seventy-fifth year of an independent India that he had fought for, Bhagat Singh Jhuggian passed away in his village aged 94. Mourners at his pyre raised the slogan that he had in school some eighty-three years ago: 'Britannia Murdabad, Hindustan Zindabad.'

Learning of his death had me recalling his last words to us as we left his home in August 2021. He insisted on seeing us off, moving quite quickly with his walker. Bhagat Singh Jhuggian wanted us to know he didn't like the state of the nation for whose freedom he had fought. None of the people running the country, he says, 'hold any legacy of the freedom movement. The political forces they [the RSS] represent— they were never there in the struggle for Independence and freedom. Not a single one of them. They will destroy this country if not checked,' he says worriedly.

And then adds: 'But believe me, the sun will set on this Raj too.'

Scan QR code for PARI Freedom Fighters Gallery.

4

SHOBHARAM GEHERVAR

MUST I CHOOSE BETWEEN GANDHI AND AMBEDKAR?

'Gandhi and Nehru did realize that they could not write the laws and Constitution without Ambedkar. He was the only capable person for that. He did not beg for that role.'

—Shobharam Gehervar, Jadugar Basti
[magician colony], Ajmer, Rajasthan

'The British had surrounded the place where we made bombs. This was out in the jungle near Ajmer, up a hill. It was also near a stream where a tiger would come to drink water. That tiger would come and go. From the fact that we would fire in the air with pistols sometimes, it learnt that it should come, have water and walk away. Else we would fire at him and not in the air.

Pic: P. Sainath/PARI

Shobharam Gehervar garlands one of his two great heroes,
B. R. Ambedkar, on April 14 (Ambedkar Jayanti)
2022, in Ajmer, Rajasthan.

'But that day, the British had learnt of the hideout and were closing in. Those were the days of the Raj, after all. So we blasted some explosives—not me, I was far too young, my older friends there—at the same time the tiger showed up for his water.

'The tiger didn't drink the water and fled, running right behind the British police. All of them started running. With a tiger somewhere behind them. Some fell down the hillside, some fell on the road. Two policemen died during that mayhem. The police did not have the guts to return to that place. They were scared of us. *Woh taubha karte the* [they had had it with us].'

The tiger apparently got out of the mess unscathed. And lived to drink water another day.

That's veteran freedom fighter Shobharam Gehervar, now 96, talking to us at his home in Ajmer on 14 April 2022. He lives in the very Dalit *basti* he was born in almost a century ago, never seeking to leave it for more comfortable quarters. Which this two-time municipal councillor could easily have done had he wished to. He paints a vivid picture of his 1930s and 1940s battles with the British Raj.

Was that some kind of underground bomb factory he is talking about?

'*Arre*, it was a jungle. Not a factory . . . *Factory mein toh kainchi banti hain* [they make scissors in a factory]. Here we [the underground resistance] made bombs.'

'Once,' he says, 'Chandrasekhar Azad visited us.' That would have been in the second half of 1930 or in the first days of 1931. The dates are uncertain. 'Don't ask me about exact dates,' says Shobharam. 'I once had everything, all my documents, all my notes and records, right in this house. There was a flood here in 1975 and I lost everything.'

Chandrasekhar Azad was among those who, together with Bhagat Singh, reorganized the Hindustan Socialist Republican Association in 1928. In 1931, on 27 February, Azad took his own life in a shootout with British police at Alfred Park in Allahabad when left with a single bullet in his firearm. Honouring his pledge never to be captured alive and always remain 'Azad' or free. He was 24 when he died.

After Independence, Alfred Park was renamed the Chandrasekhar Azad Park.

'Azad came and visited the place [the bomb-makers' camp],' says Shobharam back in Ajmer. 'He guided us on how we could make our bombs more efficient. He gave us a better formula. He even applied *tilak* at the place where the freedom fighters worked. Then he said to us that he would like to see the tiger. We told him to stay the night so that he could get a glimpse.

'So the tiger came and went, and we fired in the air. Chandrasekhar*ji* asked us why we fire. We told him that the tiger knows that we can harm him, so he just walks away.' An arrangement that allowed the tiger to have his water and the fighters their security.

'But that other day I am telling you about, the British police had got there first. And as I said, there was mayhem and chaos.'

Shobharam claims no personal role in that bizarre battle or related skirmish. He was witness to it all, though. He could not have been much more than 5 years old when Azad came, he says. 'He was in disguise. Our job was simply to escort him to the place in the jungle and hill where the bombs were made. Two of us boys took him and a colleague of his there to the camp.'

It was, in fact, a clever decoy game. An innocent looking uncle-out-with-nephews scene.

'Azad saw the workshop—it was not a factory—and patted our backs. And told us children: *"Aap toh sher ke bachche hain* [you are lion cubs]. You are brave and do not fear death." Even our family members said, "It is okay if you die. You are anyway doing all this only for freedom."'

'The bullet did not kill or maim me permanently. It hit me in the leg and went on ahead. See?' And he shows us the very visible spot where it hit him on his right leg, a little below the knee. It did not lodge itself in his leg. But it was a painful blow. 'I fainted and they took me to a hospital,' he says.

That was around 1942, when he was a 'lot older'— meaning around 16—and taking part in direct action. Today, at 96, Shobharam Gehervar seems to be in very good shape— over six feet tall, fit, ramrod straight and active. Talking to us at his home in Ajmer, Rajasthan. Telling us of his hectic life across nine decades. Right now, he's speaking of the time he got shot.

'There was a meeting, and someone spoke out "a little out of control" against the British Raj. So the police picked up a few freedom fighters. They fought back and started beating the police. This was at the Swatantrata Senani Bhavan [freedom fighters' office]. Of course, that name we gave it after Independence. Then it was called nothing in particular.

'At the public meetings there, freedom fighters daily educated people about the Quit India movement. They exposed the British Raj. People from all over Ajmer would reach there every day at 3 p.m. We never had to call anyone— they came. That's where the harsh speech was made, and the firing happened.

'When I regained consciousness at the hospital, the police did visit me. They did their work; they wrote down something. But they did not arrest me. They said: "He has been hit by a bullet. That much punishment is enough for him."'

That was not motivated by kindness, he says. If the police had filed a case against him, they would have to admit they had fired a bullet at Shobharam. And he had not made any inflammatory speech himself. Nor had he turned violent against anyone else.

'The British wanted to save their face,' he says. 'They were really not bothered if we died. Millions died across years and only then this country got its freedom. Like in Kurukshetra, the Surya Kunda was filled with the blood of the warriors. You should keep this in mind. We did not get our freedom so easily. We have shed our blood for it. More blood than at Kurukshetra. And the movement was all over. Not just in Ajmer. The struggle was everywhere. In Mumbai, in Calcutta [now Kolkata] . . .

'It was after that bullet wound, I decided not to get married,' he says. 'Who knew if I would survive the struggle? And I could not devote myself to *seva* [social service] and run a family.' Shobharam lives with his sister Shanti and her children and grandchildren. At 75, she is twenty-one years younger than him.

With his sister Shanti at their home in Jadugar Basti in Ajmer town, Rajasthan.

'Shall I tell you something?' Shanti asks us. And speaks with total calm and assurance. 'It is because of me that this fellow is still alive. I and my children have looked after him all his life. I was married at the age of 20 and I became a widow after some years. My husband was 45 when he died. I have looked after Shobharam always and I am very proud of that. Now my grandchildren and their wives also look after him.

'Some time ago, he was very sick. He almost died. That was in 2020. I held him in my arms and prayed for him. Now you see him alive and well.'

So what happened with those bombs made in the hidden camp?

'We travelled to wherever there was a demand. And there was plenty of that. I think I have been to all corners of this country, carrying those bombs. We travelled mostly by train. And from the stations, by other transport. Even the British police were scared of us.'

What did these bombs look like?

'Like this [he makes small spherical shapes with his hands]. This size—like a grenade. There were many kinds according to the time required for them to detonate. Some would blast immediately; some would take four days. Our leaders explained everything, how to set it up, and then sent us.

'We were in great demand at that time! I have been to Karnataka. To Mysore, Bengaluru, all sorts of places. See, Ajmer was a prominent centre for the Quit India movement, for the struggle. So was Benares [Varanasi]. There were other places like Baroda in Gujarat and Damoh in Madhya Pradesh. People looked up to Ajmer, saying the movement is strong in this town and that they would follow the footsteps of the freedom fighters here. Of course, there were many others, too.'

But how did they manage their train journeys? And how did they evade capture? The British suspected them of carrying secret letters between leaders to avoid postal censorship. And also knew that some of the young people were carrying bombs.

'Those days the letters by post were checked, opened and read. To evade that, our leaders formed a group of youngsters and trained us in taking letters to a particular place. "You have to take this letter and give it to Dr Ambedkar in Baroda." Or to some other person, in some other place. We would keep the letters in our underwear, in our crotch.

'The British police would stop us and ask questions. If they saw us on a train, they might ask: "You told us you were going to that one place but now you're going somewhere else." But we and our leaders knew this could happen. So if we were going to Benares, we would get down at some distance away from that city.

'We'd already been told the *dak* [letters] must reach Benares. Our leaders advised us: "A little away from that city, you pull the chain and get off the train." So we did that.

'Those days, trains had steam engines. We'd go inside the engine room and show a pistol to the rail driver. "We will kill you and only then we will die," we would warn him. He would then find us a place on board. The CID, police, all of them, sometimes came and checked. And saw only ordinary passengers sitting in the main bogies.

58

'As told, we pulled the chain at a certain point. The train stopped a long time. Then some freedom fighters brought horses when it was dark. We rode them and escaped. In fact, we reached Benares before the train did!

'There was once a warrant in my name. We got caught while carrying the explosives. But we threw them away and escaped. The police found those and studied them to see what kind of explosives we were using. They were after us. So it was decided we should leave Ajmer. I was sent to [then] Bombay.'

And who hid and sheltered him in Mumbai?

'Prithviraj Kapoor,' he says proudly. The great actor was well on his way to stardom by 1941. He was also believed to be, though hard to confirm, a founding member of the Indian People's Theatre Association in 1943. Kapoor and some other leading lights of Bombay's theatre and film world were very supportive of, even involved in, the freedom struggle.

'He sent us to one Trilok Kapoor, some relative of his. I think he later acted in a film called *Har Har Mahadev*.' Trilok, though Shobharam did not know this, was in fact Prithviraj's younger brother. He was also one of the most successful actors of his era. *Har Har Mahadev* was to be the biggest grosser of 1950.

'Prithviraj gave us a car for a while, and we roamed around Bombay. I was in that city for nearly two months. Then we went back. We were needed for other actions. I wish I could have shown you the warrant. It was in my name. And other youngsters too had warrants out for them.

'But that flood here in 1975 destroyed everything,' he says with great sadness. 'All my papers were gone. Many certificates, including some from Jawaharlal Nehru. You would have gone mad if you had seen those papers. But everything got washed away.'

'Why should I choose between Gandhi and Ambedkar? I can choose both, no?'

We're at the Ambedkar statue in Ajmer. It's the great man's 131st birth anniversary, and we've brought Shobharam Gehervar here with us. The old Gandhian had requested that we drive him out to this spot so he could garland the statue. Which is when we asked where he stood on both icons.

He rephrased what he had told us earlier at his home. 'See, Ambedkar and Gandhi, both of them did very good work. It needs two wheels each side to move a car. Where is the contradiction? If I found merit in some principles of the Mahatma, I followed those. Where I found merit in the teachings of Ambedkar, I followed those.'

Both Gandhi and Ambedkar, he says, visited Ajmer. In the case of Ambedkar, 'We would meet and garland him at the railway station. That is, when his train bound for somewhere else would stop here.' Shobharam met both of them while very young.

'In 1934, when I was still very small, Mahatma Gandhi was here. Here, where we are sitting right now. In this very Jadugar Basti [Magician's Colony].' Shobharam would have been 8 around then.

'In the case of Ambedkar, I once carried some letters for him from our leaders to Baroda [now Vadodara]. The police would open our letters in the post office. So we used to personally carry important papers and letters. That time, he patted me on my head and asked, "Do you live in Ajmer?"'

Did he know Shobharam was from the Koli community?

'Yes, I told him. But he didn't talk about it much. He understood those things. He was a highly educated person. He told me I could write to him in case I was in need.'

Shobharam is okay with both labels—'Dalit' and 'Harijan'. Also, 'If one is a Koli, let it be. Why should we hide our caste? When we say Harijan or Dalit, there is no difference. In the end, whatever you call them, they all remain Scheduled Castes.'

Shobharam's parents were manual labourers. Mostly around railways projects.

'Everybody ate only one meal a day,' he says. 'And there was never alcohol in this family.' He is from the same social group, he reminds us, 'that [now former] President of India Ram Nath Kovind belongs to. He was once President of our Akhil Bharatiya Koli Samaj'.

Shobharam's community was excluded from education. Perhaps the main reason he made a rather late entry into school. 'In Hindustan,' he says, 'the upper castes, the Brahmins, the

Jains, others, became slaves to the British. These were people who always practised untouchability.

'I tell you, most of the Scheduled Caste people here might have converted to Islam, if not for the Congress Party and the Arya Samaj of that time. Had we continued in the old ways, we would not have attained Independence.

'See, no one enrolled untouchables in schools at that time. They would say he is a Kanjar, or he is a Dom and so on. We were excluded. I only went to Class I around age 11. Because the Arya Samaj people of that time were trying to counter the Christians. Many from my caste, near the Link Road area, had converted to Christianity. So, some Hindu sects began accepting us, even encouraging us to join the Dayanand Anglo Vedic [DAV] schools.'

But the discrimination would not fade away, and the Koli *samaj* started its own school.

'That's where Gandhi came, to the Saraswati Balika Vidyalaya. It was a school started by senior people from our community. It is still operational. Gandhi was in awe of our work. "You have done a very good job. You've gone far ahead of what I had expected," he said.

'Though begun by us Kolis, students from other castes also joined. At first, all of them belonged to the Scheduled Castes. Later, many people from other communities joined the school. Eventually, the [upper-caste] Agarwals took over the school. The registration was with us. But they took over the management.' He still does visit the school. Or did, till the COVID-19 pandemic struck and all schools were shut.

'Yes, I still go. But it is those [upper-caste] people who run it now. They have even opened a BEd college.

'I studied only till Class IX. And I regret that so much. Some of my friends went on to become IAS officers after Independence. Others went on to achieve great heights. But I had devoted myself to *seva*.'

Shobharam is a Dalit and self-declared Gandhian. He also deeply admires Dr Ambedkar. And tells us this: 'I was also with both, *Gandhivad* and *krantivad* [Gandhian path and revolutionary movement]. Both were closely linked.' So, while primarily a Gandhian, there were three political streams he associated with.

Much as Shobharam loves and admires Gandhi, he does not place him above criticism. Especially in relation to Ambedkar.

'Gandhi got scared when he faced the challenge of Ambedkar. Gandhi feared that all the Scheduled Castes were going with Babasaheb. So did Nehru. They worried that this would weaken the larger movement. Yet, they both knew he was a highly capable person. When the country gained Independence, everybody was tense over this conflict.

'They did realize that they could not write the laws and Constitution without Ambedkar. He was the only capable person for that. He did not beg for that role. Everyone else begged him to write the framework of our laws. He was like Brahma who created this world. A brilliant, learned man. Yet, we Hindustani *log* [people] were a horrible lot. We treated him so badly before and after 1947. He was even excluded from the story of the freedom movement. Yes, he is an inspiration for me, even today.'

Shobharam also says, 'I am totally a Congressman at heart. A *real* Congressman.' By which he means he is critical of the party's current direction. He believes the present leadership of India will 'turn this country into a dictatorship'. And so 'the Congress must revive itself and save Constitution and country'.

He is most appreciative of Rajasthan Chief Minister Ashok Gehlot. 'He is concerned about people. He looks out for us freedom fighters.' The freedom fighter's pension in this state is the highest in the country. The Gehlot government raised it to Rs 50,000 in March 2021. The highest central pension for freedom fighters is Rs 30,000.

Shobharam maintains he is a Gandhian. Even as he steps down from garlanding the Ambedkar statue.

'See, I simply followed those whom I liked. I followed the thoughts of each that I agreed with. And those were many. I never saw any kind of problem in doing so. Or in either of them.'

Shobharam Gehervar is taking us to the Swatantrata Senani Bhavan—the meeting place of old freedom fighters in Ajmer. This is centrally located in a busy market. I'm desperately trying to keep pace with the old gentleman who dashes off into a lane, cutting through rather rowdy traffic. He uses no walking stick and strides off at quite a speed.

The only time we would see him look a little nonplussed and trying to cope would come later. When we visited the school he had been so proud of. And reading, quite literally, the writing on the wall. '*Saraswati School bandh pada hain*,' says a hand-painted notice there ('The Saraswati School is closed'). It and the college have been shut down. Permanently, say the watchmen and others around. It could soon just be valuable real estate.

But at the Swatantrata Senani Bhavan, he is both more nostalgic and pensive.

'On 15 August 1947, when they hoisted the Indian flag at Red Fort, we raised the tricolour here. We decorated this Bhavan like a new bride. And all of us freedom fighters were there. We were still young then. And all of us in a jubilant mood.

'This bhavan was special. There was no single owner for the place. There were many freedom fighters, and we did many things for our people. We sometimes used to visit Delhi and meet Nehru. Later, we met Indira Gandhi. Now, none of them is alive.

'We had so many great freedom fighters. So many I worked with on the *kranti* side. And on the *seva* side.' He rattles off names.

'Dr Sardanand, Veer Singh Mehta, Ram Narayan Chaudhari. Ram Narayan was the elder brother of Durga Prasad Chaudhari, editor of *Dainik Navjyoti*. There was the Bhargav family from Ajmer. Mukut Bihari Bhargav was a member of the committee that, under Ambedkar, drafted the

Constitution. All of them are no more. There was Gokulbhai Bhatt, one of our great freedom fighters. He was Rajasthan *ke* Gandhi*ji*.' Bhatt was briefly Chief Minister of the princely state of Sirohi but gave it up to fight for social reform and freedom.

Shobharam is emphatic that no one from the Rashtriya Swayamsevak Sangh (RSS) had any role in the freedom struggle.

'*Woh? Unhone toh ungli bhi nahi katayi*' ('They did not so much as suffer a single cut on a finger').

The one thing that worries him greatly now is the fate of the Swatantrata Senani Bhavan.

'Now I am old. And I can't come here every day. But if I am well, I make it a point to come and sit for at least an hour. I meet people who drop by and try to help them with their problems whenever I can.

'There is no one with me. I am all alone these days. Most of the other freedom fighters have died. And a few who are still alive are infirm and in very poor health. So I am the only one looking after the Swatantrata Senani Bhavan. Even today, I cherish it, try and preserve it. But it brings tears to my eyes. Because I have no one else with me.

'I have written to Chief Minister Ashok Gehlot. Appealing to him to take over this Bhavan before it is grabbed by someone.

'This place is worth crores of rupees. And it is right in the centre of the city. Many people try to lure me. They say, "Shobharam*ji*, what can you do alone? Give it [this property] to us. We will give you crores in cash." I tell them they can do whatever they like with the building after I die. What can I do? How can I do as they ask? Millions have died for this, for this our freedom. And what would I do with all that money?

'And I want to bring your attention to this. Nobody cares about us. No one asks about the freedom fighters. There is not a single book which tells schoolchildren how we fought for freedom and achieved it. What do people know about us?'

Scan QR code for PARI Freedom Fighters Gallery.

5

IN TELANGANA, A QUEST
FOR SWARAJYAM

'The slingshot was my weapon, the cell phone and the laptop are yours, as are so many other technologies I cannot even name.'

—Mallu Swarajyam, Hyderabad, Telangana

'This,' she said, 'was our weapon.'

Mallu Swarajyam was addressing an audience of 1,500 young techies in Telugu, most of them in their twenties. And doing so from a stage in a Hyderabad auditorium. 'This' was a rather nasty looking rope and leather slingshot, *vadiselu* in Telugu. And having introduced the weapon and explained its uses, the octogenarian freedom fighter began twirling it above her head with power and ease. Much to the alarm of some in the audience in closest range. The onstage translator standing behind her, researcher and activist Dr K. Lalita, ducked at the first swing, then wisely sat down.

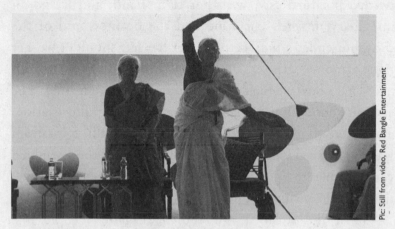

Pic: Still from video, Red Bangle Entertainment

Mallu Swarajyam demonstrates the use of the slingshot as a weapon on stage in Hyderabad 2014.

That was Swarajyam at age 84. We had made the mistake of asking her earlier whether slingshots and catapults, while okay for hunting, could really be effective as combat weapons. That had peeved her. Here she was, standing up to give us a live demo of how she and her fellow revolutionaries had used them way back in the Telangana People's Struggle of the 1940s. Against the Nizam's *razakars* [paramilitary]. Against the Malabar Special Police sent to quell the fighters. And in taking on the armed militia of the feudal landlords.

Swarajyam had even brought along a cricket ball to put into the sling and release for our edification. To the gathering's relief, she said, 'I won't use this "stone" this time, I don't want it to injure any of you. I will just show you how the *vadiselu* is used.' She then swung and twirled it effortlessly, with her right hand, and let go an imaginary missile. The rope and the business end of the slingshot ended up gracefully over her left shoulder via her right armpit.

'That's how we took on the Nizam's police,' she said. The audience burst out in applause and gave her a standing ovation. They were to give her three that day. But Mallu Swarajyam was not finished with them as yet. She exhorted the assembled young techies to fight, as she had, for a better society. For one that valued equality and justice.

Then she stunned the audience again. 'People like you have been at the forefront of the Occupy Wall Street movement. There is so much you can achieve if you will fight. The slingshot was my weapon, the cell phone and the laptop are yours, as are so many other technologies I cannot even name.'

The slingshot did not remain her only weapon. She did use it with great effect from age 13 onwards. But just as she turned 16, the Communist-led Telangana uprising gave her a rifle and trained her to use it.

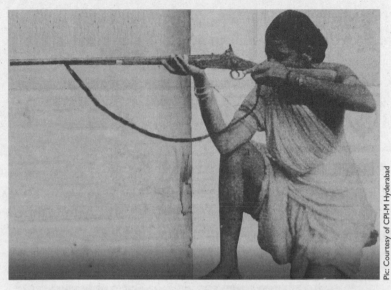

Pic: Courtesy of CPI-M Hyderabad

Mallu Swarajyam wielding a rifle in the Telangana uprising, c. 1946.

'There was a system to be followed,' says Swarajyam. 'We had to reach a certain age and show a level of competence. Only then were we given firearms. After I established my worth, I was entrusted with a rifle. The people themselves nominated me as a leader.'

It wasn't just the Communists who understood her worth. The Nizam's government did, too—and placed a price of Rs 10,000 on her capture, dead or alive. How much was that worth back then? Well, you could buy over 83,000 kg of rice of a decent quality in 1947 for that amount. That was when rice cost 12 paise a kilo. Today, the same amount of rice in roughly the same quality would cost you around Rs 40 lakhs.

The bounty on Mallu Swarajyam's head, then, was worth perhaps close to four million rupees in today's terms.

She herself was never greatly impressed by that threat or those numbers. Not then, not now. 'The people were with us,' she says simply.

She was born 'either in 1930 or 1931', she says. And isn't really bothered about the day and month. 'I began attending Marxist political classes at the age of 11 or 12, I am not quite sure which.' What she does recall with great clarity is 'the Veera Telangana Porattam [the heroic armed struggle of the Telangana people] to break the shackles of slavery and obtain justice'.

Pic: Courtesy of CPI-M Hyderabad

Mallu Swarajyam at around age 11 [bottom row right] at a *sangham* training camp in Telangana held sometime in 1942.

Soon, 'Rajakka'—her underground *nom de guerre*—emerged a key organizer and famous fighter in the guerrilla war the people waged against the Nizam and their tyrannical landlords. Telangana was easily one of the most feudal regions of India. The nature and levels of exploitation Swarajyam describes seem right out of late nineteenth century literature on feudal terror. Yet, they were very real in that region as late as the 1940s.

In a very short time, she was leader of a *dalam* (armed fighters' squad). In months, she would be leader of all 'the *dalams* in Bayyaram in the forests of Warangal, near Pindipolu'. She is talking to us now at her home in our third and final meeting with her in Hyderabad on 29 October 2021.

'There used to be a lot of sand there in Byyaram, where we would have lively drills. I used to stay there, and it was also the place where I fell ill. I was taken to a cave to rest and recuperate. Cowherds would come there to graze their cattle and would give me some milk on which I survived.

'We went on raids against the landlords and the *razakars*.' '*Razakar*' in theory meant a 'volunteer'. In practice, the bands of *razakars* served as an armed, fanatical and lethal private militia. Their common cause was to maintain the Nizam's rule and resist Hyderabad's integration into India.

Swarajyam laughs: 'People learnt to make a lot of noise to exaggerate their numbers. So, if they were ten of them raiding a place, they made it sound like there were twenty to thirty of them. They also spread inflated stories making legends of us leaders to terrify the enemy. I knew how to ride a horse and sometimes did. And was given the nickname *Jhansilaxmi*— after the Jhansi rani! That kind of propaganda is an ancient principle of warfare, you know.'

At its height, the Veera Telangana Porattam spread across almost 5,000 villages. It touched over three million lives across some 25,000 square kilometres. In the villages under their control, this people's movement set up a parallel government. That included the creation of *gram swaraj* committees or village communes. Close to one million acres of land were redistributed amongst the poor. Most official histories date the Communist-led uprising as occurring from 1946–51. But great agitations and revolts were already underway there from late 1943.

'We fought against the Nizam and his *razakars*. We fought against *vetti chakri* [forced and unpaid labour]. We attacked slavery of many kinds. We called on women to rise up not just to join the struggle but also to assert their own rights. How many young women, and older ones too, came forward to join us! Women played a leading role in many battles against the feudal forces. There were *mahila dalams* [armed squads of women fighters]. All *dalams* in our area had around eight members each.'

But she was the only woman who led all the *dalams* of her region.

It wasn't just against the *razakars* and the landlords that the women mobilized. Swarajyam and some of her fellow Communist activists 'fought against liquor and wife-beating. Against ill-treatment by their husbands. For all their rights'. She had several run-ins with some of her male comrades, who clung on to their patriarchal prejudices. Mostly, they came off a lot worse from their encounters with Mallu Swarajyam.

Swarajyam [first from left] at a firearms training camp for women
in Telangana, c. 1946.

In the course of the larger struggle, alongside Marxist philosophy,
'the women also learnt other techniques of self-defence, like
throwing chilli powder and sand in the eyes of their attackers.
They learnt to strike and fight them with sickles. We even told
women to castrate the men who assaulted them sexually.

'But it wasn't that we made fighters out of the people. It
was the people who rose in rebellion and made leaders out of
us.' It was 'the heroism of ordinary people that inspired us in
the struggle'.

A struggle she always recalls with the cry: *bhumi, bhukti,
vimukti.* Land, livelihood, liberation.

'O brave hearts of Nalgonda
Raise the red flag now.'

Swarajyam chants a line from one of the songs the revolutionaries sang. She herself was a singer—and composer. One who brought a new dimension to the *uyyala* songs that women sang in the fields while working ('*Uyyala*' means swing or cloth cradle). This seemingly innocent, lullaby-like cradle-song genre, where each line ended with '*uyyala*', she loaded with radical, political content.

'Are you devoid of pus and blood, *uyyala*?' one of her songs asked the workers in the fields.

'If you can plough the fields, *uyyala*, can you not also revolt, *uyyala*?'

Probably her most famous one was about the atrocities of the thugs of the *doras* (feudal landlords) on lactating mothers. 'They would not allow them to take a break to breastfeed their babies and even tortured one woman's breasts. I wrote an *uyyala* song about that.'

Mallu Swarajyam herself came from a background of relative privilege. 'My mother Chokkamma came from a well-off landlord family. My father Bheemireddy Ramreddy too came from a smaller landowning family that was very status conscious. With the marriage, he came to own some land. But he was certainly not as big as some of the *doras* around—whose status he coveted. He was very feudal and in competition with his fellow—bigger—landlords.

'But because of that he wanted his children, including daughters, to learn horse riding, to have private tuitions. So he did that, though he was not rich enough to send us to an elite private school in Hyderabad. All this because he saw these things as status symbols. But that worked for us girls!

'The person who mattered most was my mother. She was as humane as my father was feudal. She was so gentle, so kind. Because of the background from which she came, she had all the trappings of wealth. When she travelled to her parents' house and back, she was transported in a palanquin. She maintained purdah and was hidden from view even from the washerman or the bangle-seller.

'My mother was never part of the armed struggle or any major action. Yet, she was very progressive and was helpful to the oppressed. And she had her own feelings. It was she who named me "Swarajyam", meaning 'independence'. And oh, whenever she had to stay up during the night, she would warm up a little milk and have someone read a translated version of the Russian novel *Mother* by Maxim Gorky.

'The other very special person in my family was my elder brother Bheemireddy Narasimha Reddy. He was one of the founders of the Telangana armed struggle. He passed away in 2008. I had a younger brother, Bheemireddy Kushalava Reddy. Also, an older sister, Shashi Rekha, who served a jail sentence for three years. And a younger sister, Saraswati.'

Both her sisters died many years ago. Kushalava Reddy passed away seven or eight years ago.

From very early days, Swarajyam came under the influence of her older brother. She would, in her childhood, talk freely to the labourers and servants on their farms. It was surely from these sources that she first heard of the *sanghams* (unions, but very much a reference to the Communists). She knew nothing of them but grasped that they offered hope to the oppressed she was speaking and listening to.

Her father died when he was around 40. Not long after, Mallu Swarajyam and her brothers oversaw the distribution of a lot of their land amongst a half-starving peasantry.

Her clashes with her father, though, remain fresh in her memory.

'He built a stable near the well in our farm and raised three horses. He got me to learn horse riding along with my brother. An astrologer had told him that I was to have been born a boy, so he raised me like one. But one day, as my father was leaving for another place, he told me to get off the horse and go home. I was perhaps 10 years old at the time. When I didn't obey him, he asked our farm help to carry me inside forcibly. He then horsewhipped me for defying his orders.

'I remained defiant and told him at that tender age,' she laughs, 'that I would go and join the Communists!'

Which—a year or two later—she did.

Memories of Battle

'In Balemula [now in Suryapet district, Telangana], they had put up a police camp to contain our rebellion. We attacked the camp. It was a joint effort of the people of the village along with our *dalams*. My elder brother B. N. Reddy was the head of the *dalam*. He placated my mother, who was fearful about us girls taking part in the action. And my sister Sashi Rekha too was part of this rebellion.

'We were able to overpower the police in their camp. What's more, we got hold of a stash of weapons. We made the police an offer. We would release them unharmed if they left their weapons behind. They did, and we let them go.'

This was no mean achievement. The forces there were from the deadly Malabar Special Police, which had two decades earlier terrified people in the Godavari region. They had crushed the rebellions there, which had been sparked off and led by Andhra's most famous freedom fighter: Alluri Seetharamaraju.

'You should have heard the "toing, toing" sound as the stones from our slingshots and catapults hit the metal helmets they were wearing,' says Swarajyam. 'It made such a noise.' She gives me a reproachful look as she says this, perhaps recalling my ill-advised question about their effectiveness as combat weapons.

'Yes, the missiles from slingshots and catapults could never go as far as a bullet from a rifle. But they went far enough. In shorter range, they were very effective and could stun, even kill, a man with a head shot. We also had small country bombs.

'Plus, we evolved one more weapon . . .' she says, recalling another battle.

'In Yerrapadu [now in Nalgonda district, Telangana], one of the villagers gave us this idea: of stuffing chillies into bundles of hay and lighting them up. Then tossing them into the upper storeys of the zamindar's house where *razakars* had taken positions to target us.'

Did it work?

'It proved unbearable for them. They were unable to breathe. It was stinging their eyes and lungs. The landlord, the *razakars*, all surrendered. That main siege was a day-long battle. The whole conflict there lasted three days.'

What happened to those who surrendered?

'We took their weapons and let them off. We didn't harm them. That was always our policy. We carried these weapons on our heads to different locations.'

Were there other major actions in Warangal?

'Yes, many. In Konakandla there, we attacked the police camp. Earlier they were aiding the *dora* in terrorizing the village. There too, we chased the police away.'

What about the battles to free bonded labour?

'There were so many. The ones at Akunoor [now in Warangal district] and Machireddypally [now in Medak] were complex. What also happened there was that the police raided the villages and grabbed all the grain. When we heard of it, we gathered our forces together and went there in groups. Some led an attack. We women released the grain and snatched the tools like axes and then escaped in the melee that ensued.'

How did they deal with defeats, losses, casualties?

'We did what we could. Sometimes there was outside help. There was a doctor called Ramdas who came from Madras. He came to participate in the rebellion at the behest of Sundarayya [legendary leader of the Telangana struggle] and become one of us. He learnt how to use the rifle and in turn taught us. We learnt how to give first aid, how to deliver a child. Even how to patch up badly injured comrades till we could get them better medical aid.'

The list of the battles she fought seems endless. And with all the passion that she brings to the recounting of them, there is also a simple analytical honesty that is striking. 'Nothing could have happened if the people had not risen. It was their heroism.'

That phase of struggle came to an end with 1948. At first, people widely welcomed the new Indian government's decision to send in the army to liberate Hyderabad from the Nizam. 'Some thought that Nehru would further the cause of socialism,' recalls Swarajyam.

That did not happen. And the people of Telangana were forced to battle again to retain the hard-fought gains of their anti-Nizam struggle. This time with an Indian military that had barely come out of British control. The Communist Party, which continued with the uprising after a period of waiting, was banned in 1948. It remained banned till 1951.

Swarajyam chose to get married that same year, 1951. To Mallu Venkata Narasimha Reddy. Also a member and leader of her party.

'I did not marry as long as I was part of the armed struggle. Only after we disengaged from it. My husband was also part of the movement. He was intelligent and followed Marxist philosophy better than me. When he was part of the armed struggle, he was a *dalam* leader and an area leader. We got married only after both of us retired from that phase. I think that was the case with most of our comrades.

'My husband passed away in 2004,' she told us in October 2021. 'He was very disciplined and served as a member in the central committee of the CPI-M.'

When the CPI split in 1964, Swarajyam went with the newly formed Communist Party of India (Marxist) (CPI(M)). She would also be a founding member of the All India Democratic Women's Association (AIDWA) in 1981. Still the largest women's organization in the country. She would serve as AIDWA's Vice President for some years.

Pic: Courtesy of Sundarayya Vignana Kendram, Hyderabad

A singer and songwriter in her earlier years, Swarajyam joins in with a troupe when she's in her 80s.

Swarajyam would continue, all her life, her battle against patriarchy. She had never gotten over the way that women fighters were sent back to their homes after the armed struggle in Telangana ended. An action she condemned as both patronizing and politically disastrous. Swarajyam would never in her eight active decades compromise with patriarchy.

In 1978, her party told her to contest a seat to the Andhra Pradesh Assembly from Thungaturthy, now in Suryapet district. She did not like the prospect one bit. 'I had no idea at all, really, what an Assembly was like at the time.' But, loyal to the CPI(M), she did contest. And won—routing her own younger brother, Kushalava Reddy, who had gone over to the Congress Party. From the days she defied her father to the day she defeated her brother, Mallu Swarajyam always placed her political principles above familial ties.

'I will say this aloud: "Phoolan Devi fought against the feudal system in northern India." No leader there before her had the guts to stand up against those landlords.'

That was Mallu Swarajyam in the 2014 meeting on stage in Hyderabad. Apart from startling the audience with her slingshot skills, she wowed the young techies by bringing up the Occupy Wall Street movement. Here, they found someone who spoke not a word of English yet seemed so alert and aware of mass agitations in New York.

And aware she was. She spoke of the Occupy Wall Street slogan: 'We are the 99 per cent.' 'How can one person exploit the efforts of ninety-nine people? That was the same question we raised sixty years ago in the great Telangana People's Struggle.

'The struggle against oppression and exploitation is inevitable,' she told the techies. 'The struggle is not against individuals, it is against the system, which is really at fault. Our task is to unify the oppressed in this battle. Only then can we attain socialism. Only then can we have equality.'

On stage that day in 2014, she was a scintillating orator at her best, charming her audience. In the speaker's lounge, I got a tongue-lashing. She wanted to know why I and my generation would not get off our backsides and lead mass struggles. 'You're not doing enough. You're letting down the mass movements.'

On stage, she told the techies. 'I am inspired by all of you, by this audience. So much youth, energy and talent before me. Those laptops and cell phones—use these as weapons to convey messages of equality, of freedom of thought. Freedom from all kinds of exploitation which now happens in more subtle ways. Through corporate structures worldwide where people can't see what's happening. Where they are yet to understand that they are all slaves. In this global capital today, all of you are slaves.

'Use those skills, break the new slavery,' she urged them.

That was in 2014. In our last meeting on 29 October 2021, she had more to say.

'It looks like the whole society, and revolution too, is struck by paralysis just like how my own body has been. It's not like in our time, when everyone came together for a cause. Now they are split into so many groups based on caste' and other identities. But 'people must rebel, must struggle. There is no other way.'

Mallu Swarajyam passed away in Hyderabad on 19 March 2022. She was 'either 91 or 92'. She wasn't sure, and she wouldn't have cared. All she cared about was the people's struggle for equality and justice.

For *bhumi, bhukti, vimukti*. Land, livelihoods, liberation.

Scan QR code for PARI Freedom Fighters Gallery.

6

'CAPTAIN ELDER BROTHER' AND THE WHIRLWIND ARMY

'It is unfair to say we "looted" the train. It was money stolen by the British rulers from the Indian people that we brought back.'

—'Captain Bhau', Ramchandra Sripati Lad,
Kundal, Sangli, Maharashtra

'We stopped the train by piling up rocks on the tracks—right here where you are now standing. Then we piled up boulders behind it, so the train could not retreat. Our squad attacked the train in two groups, one led by G. D. Bapu Lad, the other by myself. Our weapons were mainly sickles, lathis and a couple of crude country bombs. The main guard on the train had a gun, but he was petrified and easily overpowered. We lifted the payroll and bolted.'

That was seventy-three years ago. But to hear 'Captain Bhau' (his underground *nom de guerre*) tell it, it was yesterday.

Now 94 [in September 2016], Ramchandra Sripati Lad or 'Bhau' ('brother' or 'elder brother' in Marathi) speaks with startling clarity about the attack he led on the Pune–Miraj train carrying the salaries of officials of the British Raj.

'He hasn't been this articulate in some time,' whispers Balasaheb Ganpati Shinde, a follower of the old freedom fighter. But memories come alive for the nonagenarian everyone calls 'Captain Bhau' (Captain Elder Brother) as he stands by the very spot on the track where he and Bapu Lad had led the daring Toofan Sena raid of 7 June 1943.

This is the first time he has returned to this site, at the village of Shenoli in Satara district, since that battle. His grandson has brought Captain Bhau's own chair from their home in Kundal, which he now places just beside the tracks. Some days, his family had warned me, Bhau can be very clear and articulate; some days, quite foggy. Holding his walking stick, he sinks into the familiar chair which, though perched on uneven ground, will hopefully give him both comfort and recall.

It works.

Today will be one of the clear days.

For a couple of minutes, he is lost in his own thoughts, then it all comes back. He remembers the names of his comrades on the raid. 'There was that Patil. And also *woh More ka ladka* [More's boy].' And still other names. And he wants us to know: 'The money we lifted from the train did not go to any individual's pocket but to the *prati sarkar* [or provisional government of Satara]. We gave that money to the needy and poor.'

Pic: P. Sainath/PARI

Captain Bhau stands by the very spot in Shenoli where
he and Bapu Lad had led the daring Toofan Sena
attack on the British train on 7 June 1943.

The amount looted on that raid—without a shot being fired—
was Rs 19,175. Not a small sum. Sure, that was the year of the
Great Bengal Famine. And though other regions did not suffer
the murderous price rise that Bengal did, they were strongly
affected too. Yet, even in a spectacularly high price year like
1943, the money looted from the train could have purchased
over 60,000 kg of rice in the Bombay Presidency.

The Toofan Sena were to make even more deadly strikes
in less than a year.

'It is unfair to say we looted the train,' Captain Bhau says
sharply. 'It was money stolen by the British rulers from the
Indian people that we took back.' His words echo what G. D.
Bapu Lad had told me in 2010, a year before he died.

The Toofan Sena (whirlwind or typhoon army) was the armed wing of the *prati sarkar*—an astonishing chapter in India's struggle for freedom. Springing up as a disillusioned offshoot of the Quit India movement of 1942, this group of revolutionaries declared a parallel government in Satara, then a large region that included present-day Sangli district. Their *sarkar*, seen as a legitimate authority by the people in the 600 villages they controlled, effectively overthrew British rule.

'What do you mean underground government?' growls Captain Bhau, annoyed by my use of the term. 'We *were* the government here. The Raj could not enter. Even the police were scared of the Toofan Sena.'

That is a valid claim. The *prati sarkar*, an amalgam of farmers and workers—with the peasantry as its backbone—functioned as a government in the villages it controlled. Led by the legendary Krantisinh Nana Patil, it organized the supply and distribution of foodgrain, set up a coherent market structure and ran a judicial system. It also penalized moneylenders, pawnbrokers and landlord collaborators of the Raj.

'Law and order was under our control,' says Captain Bhau. 'The people were with us.' The Toofan Sena conducted daring strikes on imperial armouries, trains, treasuries and post offices. It distributed relief to peasants and labourers in great distress. Emboldened by their success at Shenoli, the Toofan Sena stepped up its attacks on the British Raj. On 14 April 1944, another unit of the Sena, led by G. D. Bapu Lad and Nagnath Naikwadi, waylaid a state transport bus at Chimthana in Dhule, Nandurbar, carrying a huge sum belonging to the government treasury. This time, they lifted Rs 5,51,000. That would be roughly equal to Rs 60 million today.

In Satara, Captain Bhau was jailed a few times, early on. But his growing status saw even the jail guards treating him with respect. After all, many of them were from villages under the *sena's* control and most harboured sympathies with its aims. 'The third time I went inside, it was the jail in Aundh.' Was he tortured in jail? 'Naah,' he says scornfully. 'It was like living in a palace as the king's guest,' he boasts, laughing. Between 1943 and 1946, the *prati sarkar* and its whirlwind army held sway in Satara. As India's Independence became a certainty, the *sena* dissolved.

And I've piqued him again. 'What do you mean when did *I join* the Toofan Sena?' he grumbles. 'I founded it.'

Nana Patil headed the provisional government. G. D. Bapu Lad, his right-hand man, was the 'field marshal' of the *sena*. Captain Bhau was its operational head. Together with their followers, they dealt the colonial Raj a humiliating blow. That, at a time when similar uprisings in Bengal, Bihar, Uttar Pradesh and Odisha were proving hard for the British to handle.

After speaking an hour with astonishing clarity, Bhau falls silent for a bit as he looks around the scene of the June 1943 attack one more time. Then—'That's enough now. Let us go home.' And so we do.

The Captain's drawing room at home is crowded with memories and mementos. His own room holds his modest belongings, including a framed portrait of Gandhi. His wife Kalpana, more than a decade younger than him and no less strong a personality, stands ramrod straight in the porch as she speaks to us. She answers bluntly when we ask her what it means to be married to this larger-than-life figure.

'This fellow?' she asks with some asperity, stretching a disdainful arm towards him. 'To this day, the man doesn't know where his family's farmland is located. I, a lone woman, took care of the children, the household, the fields. I managed everything—with five children, thirteen grandchildren and eleven great-grandchildren to look after across all these years. He was in the jails of Tasgaon, Aundh and even Yerawada for a while. When free, he would vanish to the villages or run around in the jungle waving his weapon and return after months. I ran everything, I still do.'

The old warrior is sitting very close by with his hearing aid on, and so can hear what she is saying. Which he does with a half-smile and a sheepish, docile look. With that single comment, Kalpana Lad has humanized the awe-inspiring figure more than any of us possibly could in our story or in our film on him.

The *prati sarkar* and Toofan Sena threw up some of the most important leaders of India's freedom struggle in Maharashtra. Nana Patil, Nagnath Naikwadi, G. D. Bapu Lad, Captain Bhau and many others. Most of them never got the importance they deserved in independent India.

After 1947, the leaders of the *prati sarkar* went into different political streams, but most of them retained their progressive beliefs, regardless of the political force they joined. Many went to the undivided Communist Party and the Peasants and Workers Party. Some also went to the Congress.

Pic: P. Sainath/PARI

Kalpana Lad, Captain Bhau's wife, makes a scathing point
about the old gentleman's complete absence from
any work in the raising of their family.

Nana Patil went on to become President of the All India Kisan
Sabha and was elected to Parliament from Satara on a CPI
ticket in 1957.

Others, like Captain Bhau and Bapu Lad—to whom Captain was always loyal—went into the Peasants and Workers Party. Yet others like Madhavrao Mane went with the Congress. Almost all the living freedom fighters, irrespective of affiliation, mention the Soviet Union of that time and its resistance to Hitler as an inspiration for their uprising.

The 94-year-old is now tired but still reminiscing. 'We dreamed of bringing freedom to the common man. It was a beautiful dream. We did achieve independence.' And he is proud of that. 'But I don't think the larger dream was ever fully realized . . . today the man who has money rules. This is the state of our freedom.'

On the other side of the tracks at Shenoli, not too far from where we interview Captain Bhau, is a faded and sorry-looking monument. Put up not to commemorate but to condemn the great train robbery—by the British Indian Railways of that period. The text on it, if any there ever was, has been erased by weather and time. But, the old-timers tell us, there was a board or plaque that whined about the dastardly deed perpetrated here on 7 June 1943. What the Raj wanted remembered still exists. But no post-1947 memorial does, to commemorate that courageous challenge to the Empire and its tyranny on the tracks of Shenoli.

Today, the *prati sarkar* might merit a paragraph or two in some of Maharashtra's school history textbooks. The Toofan Sena was mostly forgotten within a couple of decades of Independence.

For Captain Elder Brother though, in spirit at least, the whirlwind army still lives. 'The Toofan Sena is still here for the people and will rise again when there is a need for it.'

I spoke to Captain Bhau once or twice a year ever since our first meeting in September 2016. Either every 22 June on his birthday, when his grandson Deepak Lad would call to let us wish him, or when seeking his comments on one farmers' movement or another. In 2017, the 95-year-old old pounded the streets of Kundal in support of a farmers' protest in Maharashtra.

That year, he and many other Toofan *sainiks* came to a meeting, where they were felicitated by Gopalkrishna Gandhi. It was a sight, with the old revolutionaries in tears on seeing the grandson of the man they had often strongly differed with—but still so revered.

I asked Captain Bhau then why he had gotten out on the streets to join the farmers' agitation at his age and in his health. His reply harked back to the freedom struggle. 'Then also we fought for farmers and workers,' he said. 'Now also it is for farmers and workers.'

He also sent the People's Archive of Rural India (PARI) a message of thanks for the film we made on him, saying, 'That great chapter in our history [the *prati sarkar* and the Shenoli train attack] was erased but you have revived it. We had fought for Independence and freedom, but then the years passed by, and we were forgotten. We were abandoned . . . but now the film and story have revived our pride and honour and restored us to the consciousness of our society. This was our true story. I felt very emotional watching that film. Earlier, most young people in my own village knew nothing, had no idea who I was or what my role was. Now the younger generation look at me differently. This, in my last and final years, has restored my respect.'

In 2018, an unwell Captain Bhau sent a video message of support to the November rally of over 1,00,000 farmers marching on Parliament in support of their demands. 'If I were in better health, I would be there marching with you,' he said.

On his birthday in 2021, on 22 June, I drove to Kundal from Mumbai, joined by my colleague Medha Kale, to greet him as he entered his hundredth year. I had also decided it would be good to see him once more and reassure myself that he was surviving the pandemic. The indomitable Kalpana Lad had passed on a year and a half earlier, leaving the old Captain a shrunken shadow of himself. Losing his life's partner of seventy years had drained him of that bristling energy. He was exhausted, but still sat out in the porch of his grandson's house, receiving over 200 visitors on a very hot day. Visitors, he had told us, that he had begun to regularly have after our story of 2016 in PARI revived his legend and that of the Toofan Sena.

We returned to Pune and Mumbai after greeting the Captain, saddened at seeing him so frail and vulnerable. But drove back with words of his from earlier meetings in my mind. Words he used to correct me with, whenever I sought to salute him for his role in the freedom struggle: 'We fought for two things—for Freedom and Independence,' he would say. 'We attained Independence.'

Freedom, he complained, remains the monopoly of a few.

On 5 February 2022, the old soldier faded away. A moment in history died with him. Unhonoured and unsung by the nation he fought for but venerated by the thousands who knew of this remarkable human being who, with his comrades in the 1940s, stood up to the mightiest empire in the world.

Scan QR code for PARI Freedom Fighters Gallery.

7

N. SANKARIAH

NINE DECADES A REVOLUTIONARY

'You may not know or realize that today, but the execution of Bhagat Singh was an emotional turning point for the freedom struggle in Tamil Nadu. People were appalled and so many were in tears.'

—N. Sankariah, Chennai, Tamil Nadu

When the crowds rushed out on to the streets of Thoothukudi town—as they did across many parts of Tamil Nadu—a very young boy ran out to join them. In moments, he was part of the protest, shouting radical anti-British slogans. 'You may not know or realize that today,' he tells us, 'but the execution of Bhagat Singh was an emotional turning point for the freedom struggle in Tamil Nadu. People were appalled and so many were in tears.

'I was just 9 years old,' he chuckles.

Today, he is 99 years old, but retains the fire and spirit that made him a freedom fighter, an underground revolutionary, writer, orator and radical intellectual. And a man who stepped out of a British jail on 14 August 1947. 'On that day, the judge came to the central prison and released us. We had been acquitted in the Madurai Conspiracy case. I just came out of Madurai Central Prison and joined the freedom procession rally.'

Batting on the cusp of a century when we first meet him in 2019, N. Sankariah remains intellectually active and still delivers lectures and talks. As late as 2018, he travelled from his home in Chromepet, a Chennai suburb—where we're interviewing him—to address the Tamil Nadu Progressive Writers and Artists Association meet in Madurai. The man who never completed his graduation because of his involvement in India's struggle for freedom went on to author several political tracts, booklets, pamphlets and journalistic articles.

He is one of just three surviving members from a family of ten children. His family shifted from Thoothukudi (earlier, Tuticorin) when his father found work in the Madurai Corporation. His mother was a homemaker.

Narasimhalu Sankariah came close to getting a BA in History at the American College, Madurai. But missed out on his final exams in 1941 by just two weeks. 'I was Joint Secretary of the college students' union.' And a bright pupil who founded the 'Parimelalhagar' Tamil poetry society on campus while also representing the college in football. He was very active in the anti-British Raj movements of the time.

'During my college days, I befriended many people with Left-inclined ideologies. I understood that social reform would not be complete without Indian independence.' By age 17, he was a member of the Communist Party of India (then banned and underground).

He remembers the attitude of the American College as being positive. 'The director and a few of the faculty were Americans, the rest Tamilians. They were supposed to be neutral, but they were not pro-British. Student activities were allowed there . . .'

In 1941, a meeting was held in Madurai to condemn the arrest of an Annamalai University student, Meenakshi, for taking part in anti-British protests. 'And we issued a pamphlet. Our hostel rooms were raided, and Narayanaswami (my friend) was arrested for having a pamphlet. Later, we held a protest meeting to condemn his arrest too.

'After that, the British arrested me, on 28 February 1941. It was fifteen days before my final exams. I never came back, never completed my BA.' Describing the moment of his arrest, he would say, decades later, 'I was proud to go to jail for India's freedom, to be part of the Independence struggle. This was the only thought in my head.' Nothing about a destroyed career. That was in line with one of his favourite slogans of radical youth of that time: 'We are not job hunters; we are freedom hunters.'

'After spending fifteen days in Madurai Jail, I was sent to Vellore prison,' says Sankariah. 'At that time, many people from Tamil Nadu, Andhra Pradesh, Kerala were also detained there.

'Comrade A. K. Gopalan [legendary Communist Party of India leader from Kerala] was arrested in Trichy for organizing a political event. Comrades Imbichi Bava from Kerala, V. Subbiah and Jeevanandham were also arrested at that event. They were all in Vellore prison. The Madras government intended to divide us into two groups. To one group they would give "C" type rations—given only to criminal convicts. We staged a nineteen-day hunger strike against this system. By day ten, they divided us into two groups. I was just a student then.'

It was a very surprised Inspector General of Prisons who, dropping in on Sankariah's cell, found the teenager reading Maxim Gorky's *Mother*. '"On the tenth day that you are on hunger strike, you are reading literature? Gorky's *Mother*?" he asked,' says Sankariah. The old freedom fighter's eyes gleam with fun at the recollection.

Other famous personalities were being held there, in a separate jail. Including 'Kamarajar [K. Kamaraj, later Chief Minister of Madras State—now Tamil Nadu—from 1954–63]. There was also Pattabhi Sitaramayya [Congress President soon after Independence], and many others. However, they were in another yard, another jail.

'The Congressmen did not participate in the hunger strike. Their line was: "We are bound by Mahatma Gandhi's advice." Which was: "Don't have any stir in jail." However, the government made some concessions. We stopped our hunger strike on day nineteen.'

Despite their strong differences on issues, says Sankariah, 'Kamarajar was a very good friend of the Communists. His companions sharing a room in the jail—from Madurai and Tirunelveli—were also Communists. I used to be very close to Kamarajar. He intervened more than once to try and end our ill treatment. But, of course, there were huge arguments in the jail between Congressmen and Communists, especially when the German–Soviet war broke out.

'A while later, eight of us were transferred to the jail in Rajahmundry [now in Andhra Pradesh] and placed in a separate yard there.'

'By April 1942, the government released all the students—except me. The head warden came and asked: "Who is Sankariah?" and then informed us that everybody was released—other than me. For over a month, I was in solitary confinement and had the entire jail yard to myself!'

Typically, he spent most of those days as the only prisoner, reading. And reading more.

What were he and the others charged with?

'No formal charges, only detention. Every six months they would send you a written notice, stating the reasons why you were grounded. The reasons would be: sedition, Communist Party activities, etc. We would submit a response to it to a committee—and the committee would reject it.'

Pic: Courtesy of N. Sankariah and family

Sankariah with his family—in a photo taken
around 1963–64.

Oddly enough, he says, 'My friends who were released from
Rajahmundry Jail met Kamarajar at Rajahmundry station.
He was at the time returning from Calcutta [Kolkata]. When
he learnt I wasn't released, he wrote a letter to the Chief
Secretary of Madras stating that I should be transferred back

to Vellore Jail. He wrote me a letter also. I was transferred a month later to Vellore Jail—where I was with 200 other colleagues.'

On one of his many trips to several prisons, Sankariah would also meet R. Venkataraman, the future President of India. 'He was a member of the Communist Party of India and was in jail in 1943. Later, of course, he went on to join the Congress Party. Nonetheless, we did work together for several years.'

Many of Sankariah's batchmates in the American College— and in the larger students' movement—would become prominent figures after graduation. One went on to become the Chief Secretary of Tamil Nadu. Another a high court judge. And a third became an IAS officer who was Secretary to a Chief Minister decades ago. Sankariah went on to frequent more jails and prisons, even after Independence. Among the jails he saw from the inside before 1947—Madurai, Vellore, Rajahmundry, Kannur, Salem, Thanjavur . . .

He laughs about his having done the 'prison tour' of Tamil Nadu.

He went underground once more when the Communist Party was banned in 1948. He was arrested in 1950 and released a year later. In 1962, he was among many Communists jailed— in his case, for seven months—at the time of the India–China war. In yet another crackdown on the Communist movement in 1965, he spent a further seventeen months in jail.

Pic: Courtesy of CPI-M Tamil Nadu

N. Sankariah (left) with E. M. S. Namboodiripad at a meeting
at the funeral of V. P. Chintan, veteran trade union
leader of the CPI(M) in 1987.

There's a remarkable lack of bitterness towards those who targeted him after Independence. As far he is concerned, those were political battles, not personal ones. And his was and remains a fight for the wretched of the earth, with no thought of personal gain.

What were for him the turning points, or most inspiring moments of the freedom struggle?

'Bhagat Singh's execution [23 March 1931] by the British, of course. The Indian National Army [INA] trials starting 1945, and the Royal Indian Navy [RIN] Mutiny of 1946.' These were 'among the main events that gave the battle against British imperialism greater momentum'.

Through the decades, his involvement in and commitment to the Left grew deeper. He would be forever a whole-timer of his party.

'In 1944, I was released from Thanjavur Jail and was selected as the Madurai district Committee Secretary of the CPI. And for twenty-two years, I was elected as the state Committee Secretary of the party.'

Sankariah was a key figure in mass mobilization. Madurai was, by the mid-1940s, a major base for the Left. 'When P. C. Joshi [CPI General Secretary] came to Madurai in 1946, one lakh people attended the meeting. Many of our rallies were drawing huge crowds.'

Their growing popularity led the British to foist what came to be known as the 'Madurai Conspiracy Case' against P. Ramamurti (Communist Party leader in Tamil Nadu) as first accused. Sankariah was named the second accused. And several other CPI leaders and activists were also arrested. They were charged with conspiring at their office to murder other trade union leaders. The chief witness was a cart-puller who, the police said, just happened to be nearby, overheard them and dutifully reported it to the authorities.

As N. Rama Krishnan (Sankariah's younger brother) puts it in his 2008 biography *P. Ramamurti: A Centenary Tribute*: 'During the enquiry, Ramamurti (who argued the case for himself) proved that the main witness was a cheat and a petty thief who had undergone jail sentences in various cases.'

The special judge who heard the case 'came to the jail premises on 14 August 1947 . . . released all those involved in the case and severely criticised the government for launching this case against respected leaders of the workers'.

There have been strange echoes of that past in recent years. Though it's unlikely in our time we'll find a special judge going down to a prison to free the innocent and flay the government.

Ramamurti and others were again jailed—this time in independent India when the CPI was banned in 1948. Yet the popularity of the Leftists, points out Sankariah, was high. The ruling Congress Party in Madras state saw that as a threat.

'So Ramamurti filed his nomination while in detention, before the superintendent of the central jail. He contested the 1952 election to the Madras Assembly from Madurai North constituency. I was in charge of his campaign. The other two candidates were Chidambaram Bharati, a veteran Congressman, and P. T. Rajan from the Justice Party.

'Ramamurti won handsomely; the result was announced while he was still in jail. Bharati came second. Rajan lost his deposit. The victory meeting drew over three lakh people to celebrate the win.' Ramamurti emerged the first Leader of the Opposition in the Tamil Nadu Assembly after Independence.

When the Communist Party split in 1964, Sankariah went with the newly formed CPI-M. 'From the thirty-two members who walked out of the CPI National Council in 1964, myself and V. S. Achuthanandan [former Kerala CM] are the only two members still alive today.' Sankariah went on to become

General Secretary and later President of the All India Kisan Sabha, still the largest farmers' organization in India with fifteen million members. He served as the Tamil Nadu State Secretary of the CPI-M for seven years. He was also on his party's central committee for over two decades.

Sankariah is particularly proud of the fact that 'we were the first to introduce Tamil in the Tamil Nadu Assembly. In 1952, there was no provision to speak in Tamil in the Assembly, English was the only language. But our MLAs, Jeevanandam and Ramamurthy, spoke in Tamil though the provision for it came only six or seven years later.'

Sankariah's commitment to the working class and peasantry remains undiminished. He believes the Communists will 'find the correct answers to electoral politics'. That they will build mass movements on a greater scale. An hour and a half into the interview, the 99-year-old is still talking with the same passion and energy with which he began.

His spirit remains that of the 9-year-old who took to the streets inspired by the sacrifice of Bhagat Singh.

Our first interview with Sankariah was published in the People's Archive of Rural India (PARI) on 20 July 2020. Less than a year later, Tamil Nadu voted in a new DMK government led by M. K. Stalin. One of its early actions was to create the Thagaisal Thamizhar Award, which would be the state's top honour. The prize is for a distinguished personality who has made great contributions to the welfare of Tamil Nadu and the Tamil people.

N. Sankariah at his home in Chennai. He turned 99 in July 2020.

N. Sankariah was named as its first winner. Chief Minister Stalin presented him with the award on the eve of Independence Day at his home in Chromepet.

The 100-year-old Sankariah accepted the award and thanked the Chief Minister and state government. However, he declined the Rs 1 million cash prize that went with it. That sum he donated to the Chief Minister's Relief Fund to aid victims of the COVID-19 pandemic.

This was consistent with his declining the freedom fighter's pension way back in 1972. As he once told us: 'We fought for freedom, not pensions.'

Oddly, the American College, Madurai, is yet to honour its most distinguished alumnus. Sankariah was one if its top students. He has no degree only because he went to prison for his country, days before his final exams. The college could have taken a cue from the action of the state government. But it has not to date moved the Madurai Kamraj University, under which it comes, to confer an honorary degree on this ageing foot soldier of freedom.

Scan QR code for PARI Freedom Fighters Gallery.

8

BAJI MOHAMMAD

NINE DECADES OF NON-VIOLENCE

'On one occasion, at the jail, people gathered to attack the police. [But I] stopped it. *"Marenge lekin maarenge nahin"*, I said [We shall die, but we shall not attack].'

—Baji Mohammad, Nabarangpur town,
Nabarangpur, Odisha

'We were all sitting under the *shamiana*, they tore it down. We kept sitting,' the old freedom fighter tells us. 'They threw water on the ground and at us. They tried making the soil wet and difficult to sit on. We remained seated in silence. Then when I went to drink some water and bent down near the tap, they smashed my head, fracturing my skull. I had to be rushed to the hospital.'

Baji Mohammed—a veteran of India's freedom struggle—is not recounting a scene of British barbarity from 1942. Though he has much to say on that, too. He's describing, softly and without bitterness or anger, the vicious attack on him in Ayodhya during the demolition of the Babri Masjid in 1992. Fully fifty years after the police repression during the Quit India movement when, too, he took a bloody beating.

'I was there as part of a 100-member peace team in Ayodhya.' But the team was given no peace. The old Gandhian fighter, then already in his 70s, spent ten days in hospital and one month at a Varanasi ashram recovering from the injury to his head.

It strikes us repeatedly as he speaks: A smile is his default expression. And there is not an iota of anger in him. No hatred towards the *kar sevaks* of the Sangh Parivar who cracked his skull.

He's a Muslim who heads the anti-cow slaughter league of Nabarangpur district in Odisha. The Gita, the Koran and the Bible are always on his table in the very modest residence he occupies in Nabarangpur town.

'After the attack, Biju Patnaik [Odisha Chief Minister at the time] came to my home and scolded me. He was worried about my being active even in peaceful protest at my age. Earlier, too, when I did not accept this freedom fighter's pension for twelve years, he chided me.' They had been in jail together in Cuttack in 1947 and Patnaik remained concerned about his former cellmate's welfare.

Gandhian freedom fighter Baji Mohammad at his home
in Nabarangpur, Odisha in 2007.

When the old idealist finally accepted that pension, it was to
be able to gift a chunk of it each month to a school for Adivasis
and Dalits.

Baji Mohammad is a colourful remnant of a vanishing
tribe. Countless rural Indians sacrificed much for their
country's freedom. Koraput produced many authentic heroes
in that struggle. Only four or five of the 'officially recognized'
ones, though, including Baji, are still alive. The generation
that led the nation to its Independence is dying out swiftly,
most of its members in their late 80s or 90s. Baji is closing in
on 90 when we first visit him at his home in 2007.

Just a gentle old man with a charming smile. And a firm Gandhi *bhakt*.

'I was studying in the 1930s but did not make it past matric. My guru was Sadashiv Tripathy, who later became Odisha Chief Minister.' Not that Baji lacked the enthusiasm for study. 'There was no schooling beyond Class VIII' in his native Nabarangpur. 'To study beyond that, you had to go to Jeypore some 40 kilometres away. The only way to get there was by bullock cart.'

Baji was 'No. 19 in a family of twenty children'. His parents were small farmers.

Unable to manage the bullock cart journeys to Jeypore, he moved to a hostel in that town. Through this period, 'Sadashiv guruji was an inspiration'. The British saw Tripathy—and Baji—very differently and both were repeatedly jailed.

Baji spent over three years in different prisons across the 1940s, but the first six months of those in Nabarangpur itself. In a tiny, miserable, dark and damp cell of 8 feet by 10 feet that he had to share with six to seven other prisoners. A visit to that cell many decades after still leaves you shaken and nauseous.

Baji Mohammad doesn't make much of that, though. He is talking to us about his evolution as a Gandhian. And that goes back to before the 1940s.

The miserable prison cell in Nabarangpur that Baji Mohammad
was incarcerated in, along with seven others, in 1942.

'I joined the Congress Party and became President of its
Nabarangpur unit [then still a part of Koraput district]. I
recruited 20,000 members for the Congress. This was a region
in great ferment. And it came fully alive with satyagraha.'

However, while hundreds marched towards Koraput, Baji
Mohammad headed elsewhere. 'I went to Gandhiji. I had to
see him.' And so he 'took a cycle, my friend Lakshman Sahu

also on his cycle along with me, no money, and went from here to Raipur'. A distance of 350 kilometres of very tough, often mountainous, terrain.

'From Raipur we took a train to Wardha and went on to Sewagram. Many great people were at Gandhi's ashram. We were awed and worried. When could we meet him, if ever? Ask his Secretary, Mahadev Desai, people told us.

'Desai advised us to talk to him during his 5 p.m. evening walk. That's nice, I thought. A leisurely meeting. But the man walked so fast! His walk was my run. Finally, I could no longer keep up and appealed to him: Please stop. I have come all the way from Odisha just to see you.

'Gandhi replied quite testily: "What will you see? I too am a human being, two hands, two legs, a pair of eyes. Are you a satyagrahi back in Odisha?" I replied that I had pledged to be one.

'"Go," said Gandhi. "Jail *jao, lathi khao* [Go to jail, taste the British lathis]. Sacrifice for the nation." Seven days later, we returned here to do exactly as he ordered us.' Baji Mohammad offered satyagraha in an anti-war protest outside Nabarangpur Masjid. Contributing to the British war effort, he says, was a *mahapaap*, a great sin. His protest brought him 'six months in jail and a fifty-rupee fine. Not a small amount those days'.

More episodes followed. 'On one occasion, at the jail, people gathered to attack the police.' Baji stepped in and stopped it. '"*Marenge lekin maarenge nahin*," I said. [We shall die, but we shall not attack].'

'Coming out of jail, I wrote to Gandhi: "What now?" And his reply came: "Go to jail again."

'So I did. This time for four months. But the third time, they did not arrest us. So I asked Gandhi yet again: "Now what?" And he said: "Take the same slogans and move amongst the people." So we went 60 kilometres on foot each time with twenty to thirty people to clusters of villages.

'Then came the Quit India movement, with the Mahatma's "Do or Die" call,' and things changed.

'On 25 August 1942, we were all arrested and held. Nineteen people died on the spot in police firing at Papadahandi in Nabarangpur. Many died thereafter from their wounds. Over 300 were injured.'

The shooting took place on the banks of the Turi river when British police fired indiscriminately into a crowd of protestors. More died when some of those who jumped into the river for safety were washed away by its surging waters.

Protests raged across the entire region. (In 1992, this huge area was divided into four districts—Koraput, Malkangiri, Rayagada and Nabarangpur.) The undivided Koraput district of 1936 was over 26,000 square kilometres in size. That is, over seven times the size of present-day Goa. Even today, all four successor districts are bigger than Goa, with Koraput being over twice the size of that state.

'More than 1,000 people were jailed in Koraput alone in the Quit India stir. Several were shot or executed. There were over 100 *shaheed* [martyrs] in Koraput. Veer Lakhan Nayak [also spelt as Laxman Nayak], the legendary tribal leader who defied the British, was hanged. And fifty-six people were given sentences of imprisonment.' He was, he says modestly, 'just one of those fifty-six'.

Baji's shoulder was shattered in the violence unleashed against the protesters. 'I did long stints in Koraput Jail.

'There I saw Lakhan Nayak before he was shifted to Berhampur Jail. He was in the cell in front of me and I was with him when the hanging order came. What should I tell your family? I asked him. "Tell them I am not worried," he replied. "Only sad that I will not live to see the *swaraj* we fought for."'

Baji himself did. He was released from Cuttack Jail just before Independence—'to walk into a newly free nation'. Many of his colleagues, amongst them future Chief Minister Sadashiv Tripathi, 'all became MLAs in the 1952 elections, the first in free India'. Baji himself 'never contested the polls. I did not seek power or position,' he explains.

'I knew I could serve in other ways. The way Gandhi wanted us to.' He was a staunch Congressman for decades. 'But now I belong to no party,' he says. 'I am non-party.'

It did not stop him from being active in every cause which he thought mattered to the masses. Right from the time 'I took part in the Bhoodan movement of Vinoba Bhave in 1956'. And from 'fighting free bonded labour'—despite the risks to his safety from feudal landlords.

The Koraput Bhoodan movement collected perhaps thousands of acres of land for distribution among the landless. He does not boast of it, but it does appear he was the moving spirit in that process. Nor does Baji dwell at any length on the fact that he gifted 14 acres of his own to the landless.

He was also supportive of some of Jayaprakash Narayan's social and political campaigns. 'JP stayed here twice in the 1950s,' he says. The Congress asked Baji to contest elections more than once.

'But me, I was more *seva dal* than *satta dal* [more focused on service than on power].'

The 2008 communal violence in Kandhamal district saw Baji, by then 91 years old, seeking to intervene. For him violence was 'an aggravated madness'. As he had after the demolition of the Babri Masjid, he took out *padayatras* in Nabarangpur appealing for peace in Kandhamal.

For freedom fighter Baji Mohammad, meeting Gandhi was 'the greatest reward of my struggle. What more could one ask for?' His eyes mist over as he shows us pictures of himself in one of Gandhi's famous protest marches. These are his treasures.

Nabarangpur, Fifteen Years After the Interviews with Baji Mohammad

We're peering into a foul, dismal cell.

Baji Mohammad is no more. He died on 27 June 2019, in his 103rd year. We're making a visit, on 3 March 2022, to his place of incarceration in 1942. We are accompanied by his 45-year-old grandnephew Sirazuddin Ahmad, an advocate at the Nabarangpur district civil and criminal court. Siraz follows in his granduncle's footsteps as a social activist. He heads the Nabarangpur Rajmistry Sangh (the town's construction labour union).

The locked cell we're peering into, with rusting but sturdy cast iron rods, is now used as some kind of a godown or storage space in the office of the Nabarangpur tehsildar. Chilling and intimidating even now, it must have been far more so eighty years ago when Baji Mohammad was tossed into it.

'They crammed six to eight people inside,' says Sirazuddin. There was no way that anyone could sleep properly at night for even a couple of hours. 'Their toilet was an earthen pot, used by all eight of them. Every day, one of them by turn was escorted by armed guards to the immediately nearby shrubbery to throw out the excreta of all these human beings. He would then return with the same pot to the cell. And it would be used again by the inmates.

'He told us of this and many other things on our persistently asking him. But he never complained or displayed bitterness about it. The British Raj broke his bones, but never his spirit.'

We had spent the earlier part of the evening with Baji's descendants. As many as eleven of them, including the families of Sirazuddin and his younger brother Ahmed Sharif. They still live in the old freedom fighter's home in a gulley off the Sunari Sahi Street of Nabarangpur. Siraj and Ahmed are grandsons of Baji's elder brother Mohammad Pento Sahib. Baji himself never married and had no children.

His death at age 103 saw several memorabilia hunters, some well-meaning and others not quite so, descend on the family.

Gone were the originals of the photos he treasured so much. Gone, too, the antique cyclostyling machine that he kept tucked away, churning out calls and appeals of the Gandhi and the Congress Party. 'Some people who came here told us they would go to a museum for the freedom fighters,' says Sirazuddin. He is hopeful that might still happen. But admits he has never heard from them again.

He appeals to central and state governments to ensure that such a museum does come up. That would be justice to the freedom fighters and their families. All there is in Nabarangpur is a bust of Baji Mohammad. Which only happened because of the pressure and persistence of Sirazuddin and his family.

'Even that, Sir, they have put up on a bypass road, not on the main street,' he says. 'How many people will get to see it?' Sirazuddin asks that we convey his appeal 'to both governments and society'. Which is 'that we promote the legacy of communal harmony my granduncle stood for. A harmony so much in danger today'. It's another reason he hopes that museum comes up soon.

Sitting with the family that afternoon, we could almost feel the presence of Baji Mohammad. I remembered the last question I asked him in 2007. What were his most memorable moments during the freedom struggle?

'Every one of them. But, of course, meeting the Mahatma, hearing his voice. That was the greatest moment of my life. My only regret is that his vision of what we should be as a nation, that is still not realized.'

Just a gentle old man with a charming smile. And a sacrifice that sat lightly on his ageing shoulders.

Scan QR code for PARI Freedom Fighters Gallery.

9

THE LAST BATTLE OF
LAXMI PANDA

'Because I never went to jail, because I trained with a rifle but never fired a bullet at anyone, does that mean I am not a freedom fighter?'

—Laxmi Panda, Jeypore, Koraput, Odisha

Laxmi Indira Panda did not accept the invitation of the Odisha Governor and his wife to attend the Republic Day function in Bhubaneswar. She also did not heed their request that she join them for tea at the Raj Bhavan on that day. The Governor had even included a privileged 'Parking Pass' for her car. But Laxmi did not bother to reply. Nor did she make it to their Independence Day event. She laughs as she shows us the invitation and parking pass.

She isn't being snobbish or directing any sort of protest at the Governor.

Laxmi Panda has no car and lives in a tiny room in a *chawl* in Jeypore town in Odisha's Koraput district. A slight improvement on the ugly slum where she has spent most of the last two decades. Going to Bhubaneshwar also means taking time off from her work as a domestic help. She daily cleans the homes of three families in Jeypore for a pittance. And won't be paid for the days she misses work.

Last year, she did make it to the I-Day event in Bhubaneswar since local well-wishers bought her a train ticket. This year, 2007, she can't afford it.

The only connection she has ever had to a car: 'My late husband was a driver four decades ago.' This Indian National Army (INA) fighter still proudly holds on to a published photo of herself, with rifle in hand. She never actually shot anyone with it in battle, she hastens to tell us. Her role in the INA was very different.

Laxmi (more commonly called Lakhmi in Odia) is one of countless rural Indians who fought for this country's freedom. Ordinary people who did not go on to become famous as leaders, Ministers or Governors. Just people who sacrificed a great deal and then went back to their everyday lives after Independence.

Most of that generation has died out. The few who remain are in their late 80s or 90s. And many of those are ailing or otherwise in distress. Laxmi herself is an exception to the age group. She joined the INA in her early teens and is only nearing 80 in the 50th year of Indian Independence.

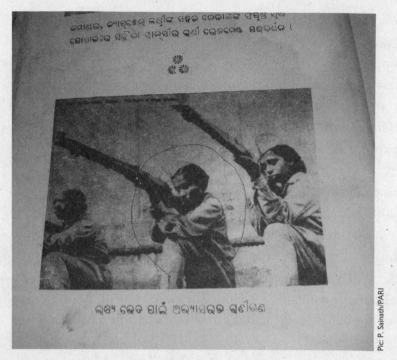

କଟାର, କ୍ୟାଥେଟେର କ୍ୟ୍ୱିକ ସଟ୍ଟ ନେଇଜଳ ସସ୍ପୃଶ ଖ୍ୱ
ଫୋଟୋଟେଳ ସଟ୍ଟିଗା ସ୍ୟାମ୍ୟାର କ୍ୟୀ ଫେଟଟେଷ ଗଟଟଟନ ।

ଲକ୍ଷ୍ୟ ଫେଧ ପାଇଁ ଅଭ୍ୟାସରଟ ବଟୀଗଣ

Pic: P. Sainath/PARI

A photo from the 1940s of Laxmi Panda at an INA reunion just
as her unit was disbanding.

Odisha recognizes Laxmi Panda as a freedom fighter, which
entitled her, for years, to a meagre monthly pension of Rs 700.
This would eventually go up to Rs 3,000. Though for many
years, no one knew where to send her the money. However,
freedom fighter status has been denied to her at the Centre
despite INA leaders of that time corroborating her claims.
Among them, Captain S. S. Yadava, General Secretary of the
All-India INA Committee, who regularly pressed her case with
the Union home ministry in 2005 and after.

Just a month before we met her in August 2007, she received a letter from the Odisha government. This updated her on the status of her application at the Centre. The letter of 13 July 2007 simply said her appeal had 'been rejected by them'.

'They said in Delhi I haven't been in jail,' she says. 'And it's true, I have not. But then many fighters of the INA did not go to jail. Does that mean we didn't fight for freedom? Why should I lie for my pension?'

And then she asks in some anguish: 'Because I never went to jail, because I trained with a rifle but never fired a bullet at anyone, does that mean I am not a freedom fighter? I only worked in INA forest camps that were targets of British bombing. Does that mean I made no contribution to the freedom struggle? At 13, I was cooking in the camp kitchens for all those who were going out and fighting, was I not part of that?'

Laxmi was one of the youngest members of Netaji Subhas Chandra Bose's Indian National Army. Perhaps the only Odia woman to have enlisted with the INA and joined its camp in Myanmar (then called Burma). Certainly the only one living. She says Bose personally decided to use her second name, Indira, to avoid confusing her with the far more famous Captain Lakshmi Sehgal at that time. 'He told me, "In this camp, you are Indira." I was too young to understand much. But from then on, I was Indira.'

Laxmi was born in then Burma, where her parents worked laying railway lines. The area they were working in had been overrun by the Japanese, and her parents were killed in a British bombing sortie while at work. After that, she says, 'I wanted to fight the British. My senior Odia friends in the INA were most reluctant to involve me in anything. They said I was too young.

'I begged to join in whatever capacity, even a menial one. My brother Nakul Rath was also an INA member and he disappeared in the war. Years later, someone told me he had come out and joined the Indian Army and was in Kashmir, but how could I even check? Anyway, that was half a century ago.

'In the camp I met Lt Janaki and saw the likes of Lakshmi Sehgal, Gowri and other famous INA fighters,' she says. 'We went to Singapore in the later part of the war,' she recalls. 'With, I think, the Bahadur Group.' There she stayed with Tamil sympathizers of the INA and even picked up a few words of their language.

She signs her name 'Indira' in Tamil in front of us, to prove her point. And proudly sings the first verse of the INA anthem: '*Kadam kadam badhaye jaa, khushi ke geet gaye jaa. Yeh zindagi hai kaum ki, tu kaum pe lutaye jaa* . . . [Step by step we march forward, and sing the songs of happiness. This life belongs to the motherland, so for the motherland sacrifice yourself].'

She shows us photos of herself in INA uniform. Of the picture where she is taking aim with a rifle, she says it was 'taken after the war, at a reunion and when we were disbanding'. 'I married Kageshwar Panda in 1951 in Berhampur and a lot of Odia INA members came for my wedding.'

She is nostalgic about her old INA comrades. 'I miss them. Even the ones I did not know well, I wish I could see them again. You know, once I heard that Lakshmi Sehgal was speaking at Cuttack, but I could not afford to go. I wish I could have seen her just one last time at least. The only chance I ever had of going to Kanpur—I went and fell ill at that time. Now where will there ever be a chance?'

In the 1950s, her husband got a driver's licence, 'and we worked for some years near Hirakud. At that time, I was happy. But he died in 1976 and my troubles began'.

Laxmi worked variously as a store helper, a labourer and as a domestic help. Always for the most meagre earnings. She also ended up looking after her son's several children.

'I asked for nothing,' she says. 'I fought for my country, not for reward. I sought nothing for my family either. But now, towards the end of this last chapter of my life, I hope at least my contribution will be recognized.'

Laxmi Panda would likely have spent that 'last chapter' of her life in obscurity. But a young journalist in Jeypore, Koraput, amended that to a new chapter—not her last one.

Paresh Rath's driver was often asking him to help out with a young friend 'Bullu', who needed to buy medicines and get some papers photocopied for his grandmother.

'After helping out a few times, I began to wonder if I was just giving him money for nothing. I decided I needed to know if this grandmother really existed,' says Rath. 'So the next time he asked for help in getting documents photocopied, I asked that the papers be sent to me. I said I would have them copied myself—rather than give him the money to get that job done.'

What he saw in those documents startled and deeply moved Paresh Rath. 'Among the papers was a book, with a list of freedom fighters' names. It was published from Ganjam district. In one picture, I saw Bullu's grandmom holding a gun.

'I found that she was getting a tiny state pension. However, she was not getting the Central freedom fighter's pension. There were papers she also had to get copied to apply for a house and a couple of minor benefits from the government.'

'I'd like to meet your grandmother right away,' Rath told Bullu. 'Well, right now she is cleaning utensils in one Marwari's house,' Bullu told him. 'After that she has to do the same thing and also other domestic cleaning chores in the house of a Telugu family.'

Journalist Paresh Rath persisted. 'They were staying in Nagarchi street,' he says. 'And one day I told Bullu, I am coming home to meet your grandmother.' And he did.

'When I went to her home,' says Rath, 'she was reluctant to speak about those papers, about her work as a domestic help. Or even about her involvement in the freedom struggle. After many requests, though, she opened a box and brought out a copper plate memento given to her by the state government long ago. It was inscribed with her name, recognizing her as a freedom fighter. But this was only the state government.'

We first met Laxmi Panda in a *chawl* in Jeypore town of Odisha's Koraput district, where she lived in a tiny room.

Why was she hiding away, asked Paresh Rath. She said, 'Look at the work I am doing. I am cleaning people's houses. I am embarrassed to tell you or anyone that. Who will think of me as a freedom fighter?'

She worked at three homes—all non-Odia families. And monthly earned 'about 300–350 rupees from each plus leftovers'.

A shaken Paresh Rath photographed her tiny, thatched 'house'. Then got it all down on video as well. 'Then I published and aired this story on 15 August. It appeared just before the Prime Minister's Independence Day speech. That was in 2003.' Rath's story on ETV Odia, and on ETV National, had a major impact on the public mind.

Still, five more years were to pass in the quest for central government recognition.

Paresh Rath moved her at his own expense from the slum to her single-room residence, where we now meet her. He also looked after her medical needs. Panda was recently hospitalized following an illness. She is at her son's place for now, despite her worries about his own problems and ways.

She estimates she is around 78 or 79 years old. She was born in 1929 or 1930. But, she says, 'I do not know the month and day.' Meanwhile, ill health and poverty have combined to crush Laxmi.

Other stories followed Rath's. And Laxmi once even made it to the cover of a national magazine. But it was Paresh Rath's

Hausabai Patil at a 2017 meeting in Maharashtra for felicitating Sangli's surviving freedom fighters—at Shenoli, where the Toofan Sena looted a British train.

Hausabai Patil [right] with her sisters-in-law Yashodabai [left] and Radhabai [centre] in a photograph taken some time after Independence.

Pic: P. Sainath/PARI

One of Demati Dei Salihan's great-grandchildren holds up a
photograph of the old freedom fighter I took at her home in 2002.

Pic: P. Sainath/PARI

A pillar-monument unveiled in 1997,
commemorating the 67th anniversary of the
Saliha revolt. It bears 17 names of people in
that uprising. Demati Dei Salihan and her
father are missing from that list.

Bhagat Singh Jhuggian at his home in Ramgarh village in Hoshiarpur, Punjab, in August 2021 at age 93. Seated to his left: Professor Jagmohan Singh, nephew of the legendary revolutionary Bhagat Singh.

Jhuggian [left] with friends, standing at the school, since renovated, that threw him out in 1939.

Illustration: Antara Raman/PARI

A young artist's visualization of Bhagat Singh Jhuggian's act of daring that saw him expelled from school in 1939.

Pic: P. Sainath/PARI

Shobharam Gehervar in front of the Swatantrata Senani Bhavan, Ajmer, which he defends from land sharks. With him are his nephew Shyam Sundar and Kavita Srivastava of the PUCL.

Shobharam Gehervar with his sister's family outside their home
in Ajmer, Rajasthan.

Mallu Swarajyam at home in Hyderabad during her last interview
with us in October 2021.

The Toofan Sena was the armed wing of the *prati sarkar*, the parallel 'provisional' government fighting the British in Satara. A photo of a Sena parade c. 1943.

Captain Bhau as he appeared in a photo taken somewhere around late 1942 or early 1943.

The American College, Madurai, where N. Sankariah was arrested in 1941, fifteen days before his final exams began. He would come out of prison only on 14 August 1947.

N. Sankariah being greeted by M. K. Stalin at his home in Chennai in 2018.

Baji Mohammad welcoming us to his home in
a gulley off Sunari Sahi street, Nabarangpur,
Odisha, 2007.

Advocate Sirazuddin Ahmed's family resides in the same
house where his granduncle Baji lived for decades.
Nabarangpur, Odisha 2022.

Laxmi Panda's son Surendra Panda, his wife Sujata, and three of their seven children, Tobbu [left], Munna and Bobby in front of Laxmi's yet unfinished house in Jeypore town, Koraput.

Laxmi Panda's most prized possession: an old INA book with her photo, going back to the 1940s.

Pic: P. Sainath/PARI

The memorial pillar for the freedom fighters
of Panimora in Odisha's Bargarh district
with the names of 32 Tamra Patra winners
inscribed (2002).

Pic: P. Sainath/PARI

Jitendra Pradhan [centre] in 2002. He outlived all the
other fighters of Panimora aka Badmash Gaon and
died in January 2022, aged 102.

Pic: P. Sainath/PARI

The temple in Panimora that the freedom fighters entered in 1945
with 400 Dalits. It still is open to members of all castes.

Pic: P. Sainath/PARI

A youngster plays cricket in the Panimora
freedom fighters' memorial compound.
'Must be somebody important', he says
of the names on the list behind him.

Pic: P. Sainath/PARI

Right up to a few months before his death, the centenarian Ganpati Bal Yadav was cycling anywhere between 5 and 20 kilometres a day on his bicycle.

Pic: P. Sainath/PARI

Ganpati Bal Yadav speaks to us of his adventures with the Toofan Sena in the 1940s.

Bhabani Mahato with 13 other members of her family, including [bottom right] her grandson Partha Sarathi Mahato, in Chepua, Puruliya, West Bengal, March 2022.

Bhabani Mahato at her home in Chepua village of Puruliya district, March 2022. Behind her is her sister Urmila, who also married Bhabani's husband Baidyanath Mahato.

Illness did not stop H. S. Doreswamy from speaking out freely to and in the media. We interviewed him in March 2021 at his home in Bengaluru.

Doreswamy addressing a public meeting in Bengaluru at age 101.

The interior of Thelu Mahato's one-room home in Pirra, Puruliya, West Bengal, March 2022.

Thelu Mahato stands beside the well he built with his own hands; next to him is his lifelong friend Lokkhi Mahato.

R. Nallakannu, better known as 'Comrade RNK', still remains active.
Here, addressing a public meeting in Chennai.

R. Nallakannu is considered
one of the greats of farmers'
struggles in Tamil Nadu.

story, followed by that of Purusottam Thakur on NDTV, that really brought her to public consciousness.

'The then Collector of Koraput, Usha Padhee, was sympathetic,' says Paresh Rath. 'She visited Laxmi Panda immediately after the story broke. She got her Rs 10,000 from the Red Cross Fund as medical aid. And handed it over herself, at once. She also assured her a piece of government land. But not very long after, Padhee left the district on transfer.

'Some people in Bengal also sent her small donations,' says Rath. Some of those, Laxmi believes, 'were probably old members of the INA's Rani Jhansi Brigade'. However, she was soon back to square one, struggling.

'And yet it is not just a matter of money,' points out Rath. 'Even if she gets the central pension, how many years will she enjoy it? It is really a matter of pride and honour for her. But the central government has simply not responded.'

'Yes, I have been allotted a piece of land,' Laxmi tells us at her room in the *chawl*. 'But how will I build a house on that without any money?' She remains far more concerned, however, about recognition as a freedom fighter than about the size of the pension that it might bring her. For the present, Rath has funded the making of a better room adjacent to her older one. And he hopes 'to move her into that new house when it comes up'.

It never did. Not fully, anyway.

4 March 2022

We're seated in a slum area of Jeypore talking to Laxmi Panda's family and descendants. She died a year after our last interview with her in 2007. Those now present include her 65-year-old son Surendra Panda and his wife Sujata. Some of their seven children are present too. One daughter of Laxmi, Renuka, lives in Bengaluru.

In the backdrop is the incomplete, unoccupied house that the old freedom fighter was given under the Pradhan Mantri Awas Yojana (PMAY).

There wasn't enough money to finish it. 'That would take at least 40,000 rupees,' says the family. They live in the same slum. Her grandchildren remember her fondly.

Her spirited granddaughter, 27-year-old Bobby, reminds us of Laxmi herself. 'We kept asking, and she told us a lot about her past,' she says. 'Grandmother told us that she and our grandfather came here to Jeypore from Belaguntha in Ganjam district.'

It was Bobby who would each month accompany her grandmother to the State Bank of India branch where she held her pension account. 'It used to be just 500 rupees when I started going with her.' Over time, 'that went up to 3,000 rupees' as the pensions were raised.

And it turns out, Laxmi's experiences were not just a matter of cooking in the INA camps. Sometimes there was no cooking at all. 'When major battles were on, they had to move out deeper into the jungles and near the rivers. Sometimes, she told us, "For ten to fifteen days we had to live on berries, raw fish, some kinds of fresh leaves and herbs. It was very hard to manage that way, but we had to do it in wartime.'"

Her descendants find it very hard to manage in peacetime. Not a single one of them holds a secure job. Bobby's brother Munna, who is 19, comes closest to having anything like steady employment. 'I work as a bill collection agent for a moneylender,' he says. 'And make 8,000 to 10,000 rupees a month.'

'Munna has been working since he was 11,' chips in Bobby. Waiting on tables and also cleaning up in small dhabas and restaurants. He, of course, never went to school. Munna was barely 5 when his grandmother died.

Surendra, Laxmi's son, is now a vegetable vendor at a nearby street market. Sujata says, 'Looking after seven children was my full-time job with no limit on working hours.' She does, however, sometimes do her turn at the pavement vendor space that Surendra holds.

So what are they doing about the incomplete house? It looks like it could be decent if properly finished. 'What can we do?' they ask.

They were granted Rs 2 lakhs under the PMAY to build this house. 'They gave us a first instalment of one lakh,' says Munna. 'We used that to put up the basic structure. Then they gave us a second instalment of 60,000 rupees. That we used to build further and put in basic facilities.

'With that we ran out of money. We had actually been spending much more than what they gave us. They would only release the final instalment of 40,000 rupees if and when we completed the plastering. And we've never had the money to do that. And cannot raise it.'

'One of our own relatives had mocked us,' says Sujata. '"What will you do with it anyway, you illiterate people?" was the question thrown at us.'

What about the plot of homestead land given to Laxmi in 2006? Paresh looks up the government revenue records online for them on his smartphone—and finds it does exist. In Kunturukhal village, some 5 kilometres on the outskirts of the city. It's roughly 1,800 square feet in size.

Usha Padhee, while still Collector of Koraput, had got the land allotted to them. They even got a *patta* (title deed) for it. But till date, after Padhee's departure, have been unable to take possession of it.

'Even if we managed to do that,' asks Sujata, 'how will we, labourers here, commute into town daily from so far off? There is no public transport that we can afford. Nor can we find work nearby to it.'

'What we need,' says Bobby, 'is that Munna and maybe one more among us, is given a secure job. That's what we need most.'

As we leave the colony, we look back at the bald, incomplete structure in front of which the family stands to see us off.

The house that Laxmi never built.

She was very pleased with the first of my stories on her appearing in *The Hindu*. It added something to the recognition that the stories of the journalists Paresh and Purusottam had brought her.

Together, they had drawn public attention to her, including that of a few well-wishers. Some would even carry her case to Delhi. There, she met President Pratibha Patil.

There were confusing reports thereafter about her receiving that national recognition she so dearly sought. Some newspaper reports claimed she did get it—two weeks after her demise on 7 October 2008. But you can't find her name on a list of individuals receiving pensions under the Swatantrata Sainik Samman Yojana (SSSY). The SSSY is the main scheme for the grant of pension to freedom fighters and their eligible dependents from central government revenues.

What we do know is that she died of illness in New Delhi while there on that very mission to gain central government recognition. She had told us in August 2007 that she was planning to take her battle to the capital. 'Netaji said, "*Dilli chalo!*" [Onward to Delhi]. That's my plan after 15 August if the Centre does not recognize me as a freedom fighter by then. I will sit down in a dharna at Parliament,' said the old lady. '*Dilli chalo*, that's what I will do.'

It was her last battle.

And a forlorn-looking statue of hers now languishes at a point in Jeypore where not many people are likely to stop and see it. Earlier, it lay at the municipal office for years till that body was compelled to put it up.

For Laxmi Panda, it was the recognition that mattered. And her dignity.

'Tomorrow,' she had told us on 14 August 2007, 'I will hoist the flag at the Deepti School here. They asked me to,' she added proudly. That was the one thing the stories on her had done. Local schools and colleges were requesting her to hoist the flag at their Republic Day or Independence Day celebrations.

'But what will I wear?' she had asked. She felt bad that she had 'no proper saree to wear on the occasion'. For decades, she had worn just the same couple of frayed, old sarees that were all she owned. Paresh Rath did resolve that dilemma, and Laxmi Indira Panda raised her nation's flag proudly then and at a few other events.

I remember her as we left that miserable *chawl* after the 2007 interview, gently humming: '*Kadam kadam badhaye jaa, khushi ke geet gaye jaa. Yeh zindagi hai kaum ki, tu kaum pe lutaye jaa . . .*'

Scan QR code for PARI Freedom Fighters Gallery.

10

THE BRITISH RAJ AND THE BADMASH GAON

'When the police tried arresting us, I said, "I am the magistrate. You take orders from me. If you are Indians, obey me. If you are British, go back to your own country."'

—Chamaru Parida, Panimora village,
Bargarh, Odisha

'Take back all these petitions and tear them up,' said Chamaru. 'They are not valid. This court will not entertain them.'

He was really beginning to enjoy being a Magistrate.

It was August 1942, and the country was in ferment. The court in Sambalpur certainly was. Chamaru Parida and his comrades had just captured it. Chamaru had declared himself the judge. Jitendra Pradhan was his 'orderly'. Purnachandra Pradhan had opted to be a *peshkar* or court clerk.

The capture of the court was part of their contribution to the Quit India movement.

'These petitions are addressed to the Raj,' Chamaru told the astonished gathering in the court. 'We live in free India. If you want these cases considered, take them back. Re-do your petitions. Address them to Mahatma Gandhi and we'll give them due attention.'

Sixty years later, in August 2002, Chamaru still tells the story with delight. He is now 91 years old. Eighty-one-year-old Jitendra is seated beside him. Purnachandra, though, is no more. They still live in Panimora village in Odisha's Bargarh district. At the height of the freedom struggle, this village sent a surprising number of its sons and daughters to battle. The records show that in 1942 alone, thirty-two people from here went to prison. Seven of them are still alive, including Chamaru and Jitendra.

'The police in the court were baffled,' chuckles Chamaru. 'They were not quite sure about what to do. When they tried arresting us, I said, "I am the Magistrate. You take orders from me. If you are Indians, obey me. If you are British, go back to your own country."'

The police then went to the real Magistrate who was in his residence that day. But that gentleman 'refused to sign orders for our arrest because the police had no names on their warrants', says Jitendra Pradhan.

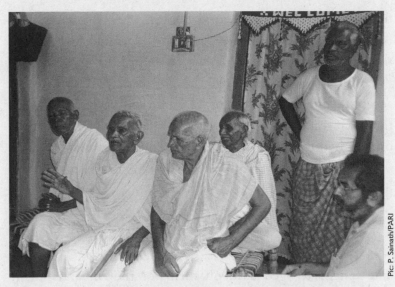

Seated L to R: Dayanidhi Nayak, 81, Chamaru Parida, 91,
Jitendra Pradhan, 81, and [behind] Madan Bhoi, 80, tell us
the story of Badmash Gaon in 2002.

'The police returned and sought our names. We refused to tell
them who we were.'

A bewildered police squad went to the Collector of
Sambalpur. 'He, apparently finding the farce tiring, told them,
"Simply put in some names. Call the fellows A, B and C and
fill in the forms accordingly." So the police did that, and we
were arrested as criminals A, B and C,' says Chamaru.

It remained a trying day for the police, though. 'At the
prison,' laughs Chamaru, 'the warden would not accept us.
An argument raged between him and the police. The warden
asked them: "Do you think I am stupid? What will happen if

these fellows escape or abscond tomorrow? Will I report that A, B and C have escaped? A fine idiot I would look, doing that." He was adamant.'

After hours of haggling, the police got jail security to accept the men. 'It was when we were produced in court that the farce reached its peak,' says Jitendra. 'The embarrassed orderly had to shout: "A, *haazir ho*! B, *haazir ho*! C, *haazir ho*! [A, B and C, present yourselves!]." And the court then dealt with us.'

The system avenged itself on them for the embarrassment. They were given six months' rigorous imprisonment and sent to a prison for criminals. 'Normally, they would have sent us to those places where they held their political prisoners,' says Chamaru. 'But this was the height of the agitation. And anyway, the police were always cruel and vindictive.

'There was no bridge across the Mahanadi those days. They had to take us in a boat. They knew we had courted arrest and had no intention of escaping. Yet, they tied our hands and then we were tied to each other. If the boat had capsized—and such things happened frequently—we stood no chance. We would all have died.'

Behind bars, the Panimora trio campaigned among the criminal convicts. The British were recruiting for their war effort and convicts were being offered Rs 100 each and

Rs 500 for their families if they joined the military. Also, the chance of being set free—if they survived the war. The political prisoners worked at getting them to turn down the offer.

'The police went after our families, too. Once, I was in jail and had also been sentenced to a fine of thirty rupees,' says Chamaru. A huge sum in a time when they earned two *annas* worth of grain working the entire day. 'They went to collect the fine from my mother. "Pay or he'll get a bigger sentence," they warned.'

The police were to get a glimpse of the gene pool the troublemakers came from. Ketaki Parida, Chamaru's mother, far from being cowed down by the appearance of the cops at her home, treated them with utter disdain.

'My mother said, "He's not my son; he's the son of this village. He cares more for this village than for me." They still pressed her. She said, "All the youth of this village are my sons. Will I pay for all those in jail?"'

At one point, nearly every family in Panimora sent out a satyagrahi. It was a village that vexed the Raj. Police and administration officers spoke and wrote angrily of Panimora being home to too many troublemakers. Its unity seemed unshakeable. Its determination legendary. Those confronting the Raj were mostly poor, unlettered peasants. Smallholders struggling to make ends meet. And also labourers and schoolteachers and *malis* and tailors and carpenters.

Pic: P. Sainath/PARI

A young Chamaru [left] with his mother Ketaki, who
confronted the police when they came to her house
looking for him and seeking to collect a fine from her.

The police were frustrated. 'They said, "Well, give us
something we can show as a seizure. A sickle or something."
She simply said, "We don't have a sickle." And she began to
collect *gobar pani* [cow dung-laced water] and told them she
intended cleaning the place where they were standing so as to
purify it. Would they please leave?'

They did.

Never mind that the history books make almost no mention of them. Nor that they might even be forgotten in much of Odisha itself. In Bargarh, this is still Freedom Village. People here took huge risks in the fight for India's independence. Very few, if any, gained personally from their struggle. Certainly not in terms of rewards, posts or careers. These were the foot soldiers of freedom. Barefoot ones at that. Nobody here ever had shoes to wear, anyway.

The old freedom fighters return to their Quit India story.

While the courtroom farce was on, Squad Two of Panimora's satyagrahis was busy. 'Our task was to capture the Sambalpur market and destroy British goods,' says Dayanidhi Nayak, then a landless resident of the village. He is Chamaru's nephew and says, 'I looked up to him for leadership. My mother died in childbirth, and I was brought up by Chamaru.'

Dayanidhi himself was just about 11 when he had the first of his run-ins with the Raj. By 1942, at 21, he was a seasoned fighter. Now 81, he recalls every detail of those days with clarity.

'There was tremendous anti-British feeling,' says Dayanidhi. 'The attempts by the Raj to intimidate us made it stronger. They had their armed troops surround this village, more than once, and conduct flag marches. Just to scare us. It didn't work.

'The anti-Raj feeling cut across all lines. From landless workers to schoolteachers. The teachers were with the movement. They did not resign; they just didn't work. And they had a great excuse. They said, "How can we give them our resignations? We don't recognize the British." So they just went on not working!

'We were an even more cut-off village in that era,' says Dayanidhi. 'Because of arrests and crackdowns, Congress activists could not come here for days at a stretch. Which meant we had no news of the outside world. That's how it was in August 1942.' So the village sent out people to learn about what was going on. 'Which is how this phase of action began. I was with Squad Two.

'All five of our group were very young. First, we went to Congressman Fakira Behera's house in Sambalpur. We were given flowers and an armband saying "Do or Die". We marched to the marketplace with lots of schoolchildren and others running alongside.

'At the marketplace, we read out the Quit India call. There were over thirty armed police who arrested us the moment we read the call.

'Here, too, there was confusion and they immediately let some of us go,' says Dayanidhi.

Why?

'Oh well, it was ridiculous for them to arrest and tie up 11-year-olds. So those of us who were that young, below 12, were let off. But two little ones, Jugeshwar Jena and Inderjeet Pradhan, would not leave. They wanted to remain with the group, and it took a lot of time to persuade them to go. The rest of us were sent to Bargarh jail. Dibya Sunder Sahu, Prabhakara Sahu and I went on to serve nine months there.'

Madan Bhoi, who is now 80, still sings a fine song in a clear voice. 'It's the song that the third group from our village sang as we marched to the Congress office in Sambalpur.' The British had sealed that office citing seditious activity.

Squad Three's aim: to liberate the sealed Congress office.

'My parents had died while I was very young,' says Bhoi. 'The uncle and aunt I lived with didn't care much for me. They grew alarmed when I attended Congress meetings. When I tried to join the satyagrahis, they locked me in a room. I pretended to repent and reform. They let me out. I went to the fields as if to work with my hoe, basket and the rest.

'From the fields I went off to the Bargarh satyagraha. I joined thirteen others from our village there, ready for the march to Sambalpur. I didn't even have a shirt of any kind, let alone khadi. Though Gandhi had been arrested on 8 August, news of it reached this village days later. That was when this plan of sending three or four squads of protestors out to Sambalpur came up, you see.

'The first batch had been arrested on 22 August. We were arrested on 23 August. The police did not even take us to court, fearing the kind of embarrassment they'd been subjected to by

Chamaru and his friends. We were never allowed to reach the Congress office. We went straight to jail.'

Panimora was now notorious. 'We were widely known,' says Madan Bhoi with some pride, 'as the Badmash Gaon [rogue village].'

Scan QR code for PARI Freedom Fighters Gallery.

11

FURTHER BATTLES OF THE BADMASH GAON

'The British promised [criminal prisoners] that anyone who signed up for the war would be given 100 rupees. Their families would get 500 rupees . . . We campaigned with the criminal prisoners [in our jail]. Is it worth dying for Rs 500 for these people and their wars? Why should you be their cannon fodder?'

—Jitendra Pradhan, Panimora village,
Bargarh, Odisha

'One day, we marched into our Jagannath temple in this village with 400 Dalits,' says Chamaru. 'The Brahmins did not like it. But some of them supported us. Maybe they felt compelled to. Such was the mood of the times.

'The *gauntiya* [village chief] Nruparaj Pradhan was managing trustee of the temple. He was outraged and left Panimora in protest forever, settling in another village. Yet, his own son joined us, supporting us and denouncing his father's action.'

That's Chamaru Parida speaking to us in Panimora, the village the British administration of the region called the Badmash Gaon. Chamaru is explaining to us that there were also battles at home in the village, too. Not just the ones against the British.

The temple entry action, he says, was inspired by Gandhi's call against untouchability. This went on alongside confrontations with the Raj.

'The campaign against British goods was serious. We wore only khadi. We wove it ourselves. Ideology was a part of it. We actually were very poor, so it was good for us.' Many in 1942 had no shirts at all, let alone of khadi.

Nonetheless, the freedom fighters stuck to their practice of creating hand-spun, hand-woven cloth for decades afterwards. Until their fingers could no longer spin or weave. 'At 90, last year,' says Chamaru, 'I thought it was time to stop.'

It all started with a Congress-inspired 'training' camp held in Sambalpur in the 1930s. 'This training was called "*seva*" [service] but instead we were taught about life in jail. About cleaning toilets there, about the miserable food. We all knew what the training was really for. Nine of us went from the village to this camp.

'We were seen off by the entire village, with garlands and *sindhur* [vermilion] and fruits. There was that kind of sense of ferment and significance.'

There was also, in the background, the magic of Mohandas Karamchand Gandhi. 'His letter calling people to satyagraha electrified us. Here we were, being told that us poor, illiterate people could act in defiance, to change our world. But we were also pledged to non-violence, to a code of conduct.' A code most of the freedom fighters of Panimora would live by for the rest of their lives.

They had never seen Gandhi then. But like millions of others, were moved by his call. 'We were inspired here by Congress leaders like Manmohan Choudhary and Dayanand Satpathy.' Panimora's fighters made their first trip to jail even before August 1942. 'We had taken a vow. Any kind of cooperation with the war [World War II] in money or in person, was a betrayal. A sin. War had to be protested by all non-violent means. Everybody in this village supported this.

'We went to jail in Cuttack for six weeks. The British were not keeping people imprisoned for long. Mainly because there were thousands cramming into their jails. There were just too many people willing to be jailed.'

The anti-untouchability campaign threw up the first internal pressures. But these were overcome. 'Even today,' says Dayanidhi, 'we don't use Brahmins for most of our rituals. That temple entry upset some of them. Though, of course, most felt compelled to join us in the Quit India movement.'

Caste exerted other pressures, too. 'Each time we came out of jail,' says Madan Bhoi, 'relatives in nearby villages wanted us to be "purified". This was because we had been in prison with untouchables.' This purification on return of relatively higher caste prisoners can be found in rural Odisha even today.

'When I returned from jail once,' says Bhoi, 'it was the eleventh-day ceremony for my maternal grandmother. She had died while I was inside jail. My uncle asked me, "Madan, have you been purified?" I said no, we purify others by our actions as satyagrahis. I was then seated separately from the rest of the family. I was isolated and made to eat alone.

'My marriage had been fixed before I went to jail. When I came out, it was cancelled. The girl's father did not want a jailbird for a son-in-law. Finally, though, I found a bride from Sarandapalli, a village where the Congress had great influence.'

Chamaru Parida, Jitendra Pradhan and Purnachandra Pradhan—the heroes of the great Sambalpur courtroom drama—had no problems of purity at all during their prison stay in August 1942.

'They sent us to a prison for criminals. We made the most of it,' says Jitendra. 'In those days, the British were trying to recruit soldiers to die in their war against Germany. So they held out promises to those who were serving long sentences as criminals. They promised that anyone who signed up for the war would be given 100 rupees. Each of their families would get 500 rupees. And they would be free after the war.

'We campaigned with the criminal prisoners. Is it worth dying for Rs 500 for these people and their wars? You will surely be amongst the first to die, we told them. You are not important for them. Why should you be their cannon fodder?

'After a while, they began to listen to us. They used to call us Gandhi, or simply, Congress. Many of them dropped out of the scheme. They rebelled and refused to go.

'The warden was most unhappy. "Why have you dissuaded them?" he asked. "They were ready to go till now." We told him that, in retrospect, we were happy to have been placed amongst the criminals. We were able to make them see the truth of what was going on.

'The very next day, we were transferred to a jail for political prisoners. Our sentence was changed to six months of simple imprisonment.'

What was the injustice of the British Raj that provoked them to confront so mighty an empire?

'Ask me what was the justice in the British Raj,' says Chamaru with gentle derision. 'That was not a smart question to have put to him. 'Everything about it was injustice.'

'We were the slaves of the British. They destroyed our economy. Indians had no rights. Our agriculture was ruined. People were reduced to terrible poverty. Between July and September 1942, only five or seven of the 400 families here had enough to eat. The rest braved hunger and humiliation.

'The present rulers, too, are pretty shameless. They loot the poor as well. Mind you, I won't equate anything to the British Raj, though. But our present lot are also awful.'

Panimora's freedom fighters still go to their Jagannath temple every morning. Where they beat the *nissan* (drum) as they have since 1942. At an early hour, it can be heard for a couple of kilometres around, they say.

But on Fridays, the freedom fighters try to gather at 5.17 p.m. Because 'it was on Friday that Gandhi was murdered.' At 5.17 p.m. It's a tradition this village has kept alive for fifty-four years.

It's a Friday today, and we accompany them to the temple. Four of the seven living freedom fighters are present. Chamaru, Dayanidhi, Madan and Jitendra. Three others, Chaitanya, Chandrashekar Sahu and Chandrashekar Parida, are out of the village just now.

The foyer of the temple is packed with people who sing Gandhi's favourite *bhajans*. 'In 1948,' says Chamaru, 'many in this village shaved their heads when the news of the Mahatma's murder came. They felt they had lost their father. And to this day, many fast on Fridays.'

Panimora was and is a village of small and marginal farmers and labourers. And also schoolteachers, *malis*, landless people, cowherds, tailors and carpenters.

There is a rendering of Gandhi's favourite *bhajans* starting every Friday at 5.17 p.m. in the Badmash Gaon. Gandhi was assassinated at that precise time on a Friday.

It is also a village with a sense of its history, a sense of its own heroism. One that feels a duty to keep the flame of freedom alive.

'There were around hundred Kulta [cultivator caste] families. About eighty Odia [also cultivators]. Close to fifty Saura Adivasi households, ten goldsmith-caste families. And a fewer number of Goud [Yadav] families and Dalit households and so on,' says Dayanidhi Nayak. He admits it is 'true, that we have not had too many inter-caste marriages. But relations between the groups have always been fine since the days of the freedom struggle. The temple is still open to all. The rights of all are respected'.

There are a few who feel some of their rights have not been recognized. Dibitya Bhoi is one of them. 'I was very young, and I was badly thrashed by the British,' he says. Bhoi was then 13. But since he was not sent to prison, his name did not make it to the official list of freedom fighters. Some others were also badly beaten up by the British but ignored in the official record because they did not go to prison.

That colours the names on the *stambh* or pillar to commemorate the freedom fighters. Only the names of those who went to jail in 1942 are there. But no one disputes their right to be there. Just sadly, the way the official recording of 'freedom fighters' went, it left out others who also deserved recognition.

August 2002, sixty years later, and Panimora's freedom fighters are at it again.

This time Madan Bhoi—the poorest of the seven, now owning half an acre of land—and his friends are sitting on a *dharna*. This is just outside the Sohela block telephone office. 'Imagine,' says Bhoi, 'after all these decades, this village of ours does not have a telephone.'

So, on that demand, 'we sat on a *dharna*. The Sub-Divisional Officer (SDO) said he had never heard of our village,' he laughs. 'This is blasphemy if you live in Bargarh. This time, funnily, the police came in on the right side'.

The police, who knew these seven as living legends, marvelled at the SDO's ignorance. And were quite worried about the condition of the 80-year-olds. 'In fact, some hours into the *dharna*, the police, a doctor, medical staff and others intervened. Then the telephone people promised us an instrument by 15 September. Let us see.'

Once again, Panimora's fighters were struggling for others. Not for themselves. What did they ever get out of their struggles for themselves?

'Freedom,' says Chamaru.

For you and me.

Twenty Years After in Panimora

The Magnificent Seven are gone. Jitendra Pradhan, the last of them to survive the preceding two decades, is no more. 'He died on 21 January 2022,' says his nephew Kishore Chandra Pradhan, who is 78. 'He was 102.' Jitendra was a small farmer owning no more than two acres. 'Just four days earlier, he ate a fine, hearty meal,' says his daughter-in-law Noora Pradhan. Jitendra, his relatives tell us, remained self-sufficient to his last days, seeking nobody's help to get about or feed himself.

He was actually given a guard of honour at his funeral, say his relatives. One ordered by the Naveen Patnaik government, for which they are grateful. And Ministers and district officials were among the mourners. Which is nice, if a bit late.

We also meet Chamaru Parida's sons, Gagan Bihari Parida, who is 82, and Subira Parida, who is 76. Both are retired teachers. From them we learn more about how their grandmother Ketaki Parida confronted the police party that descended on her home.

The sons of Chamaru Parida, Gagan Bihari Parida, 82, and Subira Parida, 76, speak to us at their home in Panimora, Odisha, in March 2022.

'We became teachers because of Chamaru's encouragement. He wanted us to bring education to the village's children. An education he could never have himself.'

As we leave Panimora, we stop at the monument to the village's participation in the struggle for India's Independence. We had been there in 2002 as well, but it has been neatened up, built around with better walls.

There are children playing cricket inside the enclosed space with a zest and joy that is infectious. One handsome young boy hits the ball out of the park and gives himself a hearty clap. The 'wicket' at one end is the base of the *stambh* or memorial pillar to the thirty-two 'officially recorded' freedom fighters of Panimora.

'Who are these people, the names we see on the *stambh*?' my friend and colleague Purusottam Thakur asks the boys.

'Must be somebody important,' says the young batsman with a charming smile.

The newest generation of the Badmash Gaon have lost track of their most famous ones.

Scan QR code for PARI Freedom Fighters Gallery.

12

GANPATI YADAV'S GRIPPING
LIFE CYCLE

'We would tie up the ankles of the informer after placing a
wooden stick between them. He was then held upside down
and beaten on the soles of his feet with sticks.'

—Ganpati Bal Yadav, Ramapur village,
Sangli, Maharashtra

We were late. 'Ganpati Bal Yadav has already come across
from his village twice, looking for you,' said Sampat More,
our journalist friend in Shirgaon. 'He returned both times to
his own village in Ramapur. He'll be back a third time when
we tell him you've reached.' The two villages are 5 kilometres
apart, and Ganpati Yadav covers the distance on a bicycle. But
three round trips would mean 30 kilometres, on a summer's

day in mid-May, on a 'road' that is mostly dirt track, with a cycle a quarter of a century old.

And a cyclist aged 97.

Ganpati Bal Yadav with his ancient bicycle. He tells us,
'There were long discussions on this fascinating
technology when it first came to our village.'

As we readied for lunch at the house of More's grandfather in Shirgaon, a village in Kadegaon block of Maharashtra's Sangli district, Ganpati Bal Yadav rode up nonchalantly on his bike. He was puzzled when I apologized profusely for having him cover such distances in the sun. 'Hardly matters,' he said with his mild tone and gentle smile. 'I went to Vita yesterday afternoon for a wedding. There too, on my cycle. It's how I get about.' A round trip from Ramapur to Vita would have meant 40 kilometres. And the previous day was much hotter, with the temperature in the mid-40°Cs.

'A year or two ago, he rode up to Pandharpur and back, nearly 150 kilometres,' Sampat More tells us. 'Nowadays he is not doing that kind of distance.'

Ganpati Yadav, born in 1920, was a freedom fighter in the ranks of the Toofan Sena (Whirlwind Army), the armed wing of the *prati sarkar* or provisional, underground government of Satara, Maharashtra, which declared independence from British rule in 1943. The *prati sarkar* had nearly 600 (or more) villages under its control. He took part in the Toofan Sena's rebellions against the Raj.

'I was mostly a courier, taking messages and meals to revolutionaries hiding in the forests,' he says. Several of those long, dangerous journeys were on foot. Later, came those on a cycle.

Ganpati Yadav was and remains an active farmer. In the recent rabi season, he raised 45 tons of sugarcane on his half acre. He owned close to 20 acres of land earlier but divided that up amongst his children long ago. His sons have nice homes on the same property where he resides. But Ganpati Yadav and his 85-year-old wife Vatsala—a still-active homemaker who cooks and cleans daily—prefer to live in a spartan dwelling, essentially consisting of one central room. Vatsala was away from the village when we visited.

Ganpati Yadav's modesty meant that his children learnt late of his role as a freedom fighter. His older son, Nivrutti, grew up on the farm but left at age 13 to train as a goldsmith in Erode and then Coimbatore in Tamil Nadu. 'I knew nothing of his role in the freedom struggle,' he says. 'I only got to know when G. D. Bapu Lad [a legendary leader of the *prati sarkar*] asked me if I knew of my father's courage.' Bapu Lad, says Ganpati Yadav, was his mentor and guide. 'He found me a bride, arranged our marriage,' he recalls. 'Later, I followed him in the Shetkari Kamgar Paksha [Peasants and Workers Party of India]. We remained connected to the end of his days.'

'When I was in Class VII, my friend's father told me of his bravery,' says Mahadeo, another son of his. 'At that time, my attitude was—it was no big deal. He hadn't killed any British soldiers or police. Only later did I learn the importance of his role.'

His regular function was that of a courier. But Ganpati Bal Yadav was also part of the teams that pulled off the great train robbery at Shenoli in Satara in June 1943, led by Bapu Lad and Toofan Sena founder 'Captain Bhau'.

'Four days before the attack on the train, we came to know that we had to pile up rocks on the tracks.'

Did the attack party know this was a train carrying a British payroll? 'Our leaders were aware of this. People who were working in the railways and government had tipped them off. We came to know when we started looting the train.'

And how many attackers were there?

'Who counted at that time? Within minutes, we had made piles of rocks and stones that we dumped on the tracks. We also quickly placed boulders behind the train when it stopped.

So, it could not retreat. Then we encircled it, opened the doors and entered. Those inside didn't move or resist as we looted the train.

'Please know we did this to damage the Raj, not for the money.'

Outside of such militant operations, Ganpati Bal Yadav's role as a courier was also complicated. 'I delivered food to our leaders hiding in the forest. I would go to meet them at night. Usually, there were ten to twenty people with the leader. The British Raj had declared a shoot-at-sight order against these underground fighters. We had to travel by hidden ways and long, circuitous routes to reach them. Otherwise, we could have been shot by police.'

'We also punished police informers within our villages,' says Ganpati Yadav. And goes on to explain how the *prati sarkar*, or provisional government, came to also be called the '*patri sarkar*'. The Marathi word *patri*, in that context, refers to a wooden stick. 'When we discovered one of these police agents, we encircled his home at night. We would take the informer and an associate of his outside the village.

'We would tie up the ankles of the informer after placing a wooden stick between them. He was then held upside down and beaten on the soles of his feet with sticks. We touched no other part of his body. Just the soles.' No visible marks were there on the body from the feet up. But 'he couldn't walk normally for many days'. A powerful disincentive. And so came the name *patri sarkar*. 'After that we would load him on the back of his associate who would carry him home.

'We meted out punishments in villages such as Belavade, Nevari and Tadsar. One informer called Nanasaheb stayed in Tadsar village in a big bungalow, which we broke into at night. We found only women sleeping. But then we saw one woman in a corner, covering herself in a sheet. Why was this woman sleeping separately? Of course, it was him, and we carried him away in that very sheet.'

Nana Patil (the head of the provisional government) and Bapu Lad were his heroes. 'What a man Nana Patil was—tall, huge, fearless. What inspiring speeches he used to give! He was often invited by the big people around here but would only stay in smaller homes. Some of those bigger people were British agents.' The leaders 'told us not to be scared of the government; that if we united and joined the struggle in large numbers, we could free ourselves of the Raj'. Ganpati Yadav and about 100–150 others in this village joined the Toofan Sena.

Even then, he had heard of M. K. Gandhi, though 'I never got to see him. I once saw Jawaharlal Nehru when the industrialist S. L. Kirloskar brought him to this region. And, of course, we had all heard of Bhagat Singh'.

Ganpati Bal Yadav was born into a farming family and had only one sibling, a sister. His parents died when he was very young, and the children moved to a relative's house. 'I attended maybe the first three to four years of school and then dropped out to work in the fields.' Even while in school, 'I would attend for a little while and then I would go home and take the buffaloes for grazing. I can understand words and can write my name'.

After his marriage, he shifted back to his parents' dilapidated house and their tiny farm. He has no photographs from his early life and couldn't afford to have any taken.

However, he worked extremely hard—and at 97, still does. 'I learnt how to make *gool* [jaggery in Marathi] and sold it across the district. We spent our money on educating the children. Once educated, they left for Mumbai and started earning on their own. They were even sending us money. Then I shut down the jaggery business and invested in more farmland. In time, our farm prospered.'

But Ganpati Yadav is unhappy with how today's farmers are sinking under the burden of debt. 'We got *swarajya* [Independence], but things are not what we were expecting.' He feels the current national and state governments of 2018 are worse than the previous ones, which were also bad. 'No telling what they'll do next,' he says. People had lofty hopes of the present dispensation, he says. 'But everything has turned out to be the opposite.'

Though much of his courier work for the Toofan Sena in the earlier years was done on foot, Ganpati Yadav 'learnt cycling around the age of 20'. That became a mode of transport in the latter part of his underground work. 'The cycle was a novelty in our times.' There were lengthy discussions in the village, he says, on this fascinating new technology. 'I learnt how to ride it on my own, falling innumerable times.'

It's late afternoon, and the nonagenarian has been up since before 5 a.m. But he seems to have enjoyed speaking to us for hours and shows no tiredness. The one time he frowns is when I ask him how old his cycle is. 'This one?' It's 'only' about a quarter of a century old.

'The last one I had for about fifty-five years, but somebody stole it,' he says sadly. We wonder if that someone had been a shady antiques dealer.

Ganpati Yadav with his family including children, grandchildren and great-grandchildren.

As we leave, he clasps my hands tightly and asks me to wait a moment. He wants to give me something, he says, and disappears into his little abode. There he picks up a small vessel, opens a pot and dips it in. Then he steps out and gives me a cup of fresh milk. When I've had that, he clasps my hands again, tightly, his eyes moist with tears. My own are welling up, too. No further words are needed or spoken. I depart knowing I was privileged to be, however briefly, part of Ganpati Bal Yadav's wonderful cycle of life.

Sampat tells me that every time he ran into the old gentleman for the next two years, he would speak of us. The People's Archive of Rural India (PARI) 'made me famous. I was a nobody. Just a courier in the freedom struggle. But they saw my role as important and treated me with such great respect'. Ganpati Yadav was deeply touched—and this was so important to him—by the recognition PARI had brought him in his own village and region.

No one portrayed those last moments of our 2018 meeting better than journalist Sampat More. As he wrote, I 'was speaking in English, while Ganpat Dada spoke in Marathi. But when it was time to part, Dada, who cannot understand English, knew only from the body language that this man is now going. Dada was overcome with emotion. He stood up and held sir's hand in his own and held it tight. Dada's eyes were brimming. We could see that both men spoke without the need of any language'.

Ganpati Bal Yadav cycled off into the sunset on 14 April 2021. The freedom fighter and underground courier for revolutionaries had completed his century and was batting well on 101. But, after a brief illness, the man who did anywhere between 5 to 20 kilometres a day on his ancient bicycle right to his last months pedalled off to that great velodrome in the sky.

Scan QR code for PARI Freedom Fighters Gallery.

13

BHABANI MAHATO

FEEDING THE REVOLUTION IN PURULIYA

'All responsibilities were mine. I did all the chores. I took care of everything. Everything. I ran the family. I looked after everybody in 1942–43 when all those incidents happened.'

—Bhabani Mahato, Chepua village, Puruliya,
West Bengal

'It must have been very hard for you when your husband Baidyanath was jailed for thirteen months in the Quit India movement?' I ask Bhabani Mahato in Puruliya. 'Running such a large joint family and . . .'

'It was much worse when he came back home,' she says calmly but firmly. 'It meant he would keep bringing his friends, or I had to cook for them and they would pick up the food. Sometimes five, ten, twenty or more people. I never had a moment's rest.'

'But surely, your association with the Quit India stir . . .'

'What did I have to do with that, or anything like that?' she asks. 'I had nothing to do with the struggle, my husband Baidyanath Mahato did. I was just too busy looking after a big family, all those people, how much cooking I had to do—every day the cooking increased!' says Bhabani. 'Remember, I also ran the farm.'

We are crestfallen. The disappointment likely showing on our faces. We had come quite a distance to this remote part of West Bengal in search of still-living freedom fighters. And here was this great candidate for that role, in Chepua village of Manbazar I block, disavowing any connection with the historic struggle that brought India its independence.

Bhabani Mahato speaks with great clarity and decisiveness for one who is anywhere between 101 and 104 years old. Documenting the age of poor people in remote rural regions is tricky at the best of times. A century ago, when she was born, it was mostly non-existent. But we do arrive at that estimate of Bhabani's age. Via her late husband's records, and from members of her large family, including a son in his 70s. And from her slightly younger contemporaries in the few villages we are visiting in Puruliya (also spelt as Purulia).

This is, at any rate, a more reliable reckoning than the arbitrary ages handed out to people of her generation by the dysfunctional Aadhaar card system here. There, Bhabani has been assigned a birth year of 1925. That would make her 97.

Pic: P. Sainath/PARI

Bhabani Mahato makes a forceful point while speaking to us at her home in Chepua, Puruliya district, West Bengal, in March 2022.

Her family says she is 104 years old. Baidyanath, who was four or five years older than her, died in 2002.

'We had a large joint family,' she says. 'All responsibilities were mine. I did all the chores. I took care of everything. Everything. I ran the family. I looked after everybody in 1942–43 when all those incidents happened.' Bhabani does not name the 'incidents'. But they included, among others, the Quit India stir. And the famous 30 September 1942 attempt by freedom fighters to hoist the tricolour at twelve police stations in what was even then one of the most deprived regions of Bengal.

A district in which, even today, a third of all families live below the poverty line. And which still reports the highest levels of poverty in West Bengal. Bhabani's huge family held—and still does—some acres of land. That made them relatively better off than several others.

Her husband Baidyanath Mahato was a local leader. He was actively involved in anti-British Raj actions. As two still-living freedom fighters in Puruliya, Thelu Mahato and Lokkhi Mahato, tell us in Pirra village, it took a long time for news of any sort to reach the remote regions.

'Here, we got to know of the Quit India call maybe a month after it was made,' says Thelu Mahato.

And so the action planned in response happened on 30 September 1942. Fifty-three days after Gandhi's call for the British to 'Quit India' at the Gowalia Tank Maidan in Mumbai on 8 August 1942. Baidyanath was arrested in the crackdown and suffered in the repression that followed. He was to become a schoolteacher after Independence. Teachers back then played a key role in political mobilization. A role that would be carried over into independent India for some decades.

Bhabani ran the family's farm for decades, right from preparing the soil for sowing to supervising the labour and the harvesting. She even transported the produce back home herself.

There were various forces involved in the attempt to occupy the police stations and hoist the flag on them. There was a public just fed up with the exploitative British rule. There were others from diverse backgrounds. There were Leftist revolutionaries and Gandhians. And even people like Thelu and Lokkhi Mahato who we realized were, like so many others, Leftist by persuasion and Gandhian by personality.

Their politics, their passion, was with the Left. Their moral codes and lifestyle were guided by Gandhi. They were often torn between these two paths. They believed in ahimsa but at times retaliated against the British in violence. They say, 'Look, they opened fire on us. Of course, people would retaliate when they saw their friends, family or comrades shot by police before their eyes.' Both Thelu and Lokkhi are Kurmis.

Bhabani's family are also Kurmis, the largest community in the Jangalmahal region of West Bengal.

The British Raj listed them as a Scheduled Tribe in 1913. However, it dropped them from that group in the 1931 Census. In the India of 1950, they were, oddly, listed as OBCs. Restoration of their tribal status remains a major demand of the Kurmis in this state.

Kurmis were also at the forefront of the freedom struggle here. Scores of them took part in the march on the twelve police stations in the last two days of September 1942.

Baidyanath Mahato, a firm advocate of *swadeshi*, was among the marchers. His own, relatively better-off parents were worried by his politics. They did not want him involved in any anti-British Raj actions.

'Baidyanath spent the next thirteen months in jail,' says his son Shyam Sundar Mahato, in his 70s. 'He was held in the Bhagalpur Camp Jail.' Which was when we asked Bhabani that question about his incarceration being hard on her. And got her startling reply about its being much worse when he came back home.

'It meant more people coming. More folk to be fed. More people to be looked after. I cried a lot when he came back and expressed my anger that all his great heroism was happening at my expense, at the cost of his family. And with his return, my work increased.'

We refocus our attention on Bhabani. Did Gandhi have an impact on her thinking? How did she feel about satyagraha and ahimsa?

Calm though she is, Bhabani is both expressive and articulate. She gives us a gentle look that somehow conveys the impression that she is explaining herself to dim-witted children who simply do not get it.

'Gandhi . . . what do you mean?' she asks. 'What do you mean? Do you think I was going to sit and think about that and ponder these issues? Every day the number of people were growing whom I had to cater to, serve, look after, cook for,' she says, waving an arm at us for emphasis.

'Please understand, I was 9 years old when I was married. Where was I thinking about such great matters then? After that I was single-handedly looking after a huge joint family for decades. Please know that I ran the farm. From preparing the soil, to sowing, to supervising the *munish* [labour], weeding, to harvesting . . .' She then provided cooked food to the farm labourers.

She also transported the produce back to her home from fields that were quite on the edge of the forests.

And did all that in an era where she had no mechanical devices—electrical ones were unheard of at that time. And all the physical labour she did in the fields was with incredibly old tools and implements that were—and still are—designed for larger, male hands. This, in a highly drought-prone region swamped in inequality and hunger.

Some three decades after her wedding to Baidyanath, he married again. This time he wed Bhabani's own sister, Urmila, younger to her by almost twenty years. An event their relatives say was brought on by a major crisis.

A wedding had been fixed for Urmila, then perhaps 15 years old, in their village. It was the monsoon season. A flash flood in the region meant the bridegroom's party was unable to cross the nearby river. And so the auspicious *lagna* moment in the marriage was lost. A deeply superstitious society saw this as an ill omen damning Urmila—but of course not her betrothed. It also meant that no one would ever marry her.

Urmila's father had died a few days after her birth—so this was viewed as the second omen. A warning to all men to stay away. She was already living with Bhabani as their mother, too, had died when Urmila was still a young girl. Baidyanath married Urmila, the family says, to still the prejudice that haunted her.

Each sister bore three children.

Pic: Courtesy of family of Bhabani Mahato

Bhabani Mahato (centre) with her husband Baidyanath and sister Urmila
in the 1980s. There are no family pictures from the earlier periods.

It slowly sinks in. Bhabani Mahato grew, harvested and
transported the food that she then cooked for her family—and
for many others. She was doing that through the late 1920s
and the 1930s. And through the 1940s as well.

Details of how many acres she worked on are a bit hazy.
The family cultivated land, which they saw as their own but
held no title deeds for it. They worked on it at the pleasure of
the zamindar. Her huge household of over twenty members
lived off land held by both Bhabani's own family in Janra and
in her marital home in Chepua. In both villages that totalled
nearly 30 acres.

The brutal burden of work falling on her consumed every
waking hour. And those were many.

So, was she up by 4 a.m.?

'Long before that,' she scoffs, 'long before that.' It seems like she was up latest by 2 a.m. 'And I never once got to sleep before 10 in the night. Usually, a lot later.'

Her first child died after a bad bout of dysentery. 'We went to a healer, a fakir called Kaviraj. But it did not help. She was just one year old when she died.'

I try asking her again about Gandhi and the movement. 'After I became a mother,' she says, 'I could not find the time to run the *charkha* and all those kinds of things which I was doing.' She reminds us once again—'I was 9 when I got married.'

But thereafter, given the times she lived in, the troubles she pulled through, surely Bhabani can talk to us of three overwhelming experiences she encountered in that era?

'I was overwhelmed every moment. Please understand what my life was like. What do you think I was going to sit and think about? I was looking at how to manage, how to run this huge household. Baidyanath and others were involved in the struggle. I fed everybody.'

What did she do when the bruising load and stifling pressure got to her?

'I sat with my mother and cried there. Mind you, when I had to cook for more and more people that Baidyanath brought with him—I was not irritated. I just felt like crying.'

She repeats those words, wanting us to understand her well—'I was not irritated, I just felt like crying.'

And just as we're rising from our chairs to leave, her grandson Partha Sarathi Mahato, who is—like Baidyanath was—a teacher, asks us to remain seated. 'Partha *da*' has just a few words to say to us.

And the penny drops.

Who were those people she kept cooking for other than her large family? Who were the sometimes five–ten–twenty people whom Baidyanath kept getting her to prepare meals for?

'Those meals she cooked were for the revolutionaries,' says Partha *da*. 'Those in the underground resistance, often on the run or hiding in the forest.'

We sat there in silence some moments. Completely overwhelmed by the sheer sacrifice of this woman who never had a moment to herself, for herself, in almost her entire life from age 9.

If what she did in the 1930s and 1940s wasn't participation in the freedom struggle, what was?

Her son and others look at us, surprised that we had not understood this. They had taken it for granted that we knew.

Did Bhabani know what she was doing and for whom?

Well, actually, yes. She just did not know their names or recognize them as individuals. Baidyanath and his fellow rebels organized the transfer of food cooked by the village women to those on the run, in a way aimed at protecting both as best they could.

Partha *da*, who has researched the situation in Puruliya of that time, would explain to us later: 'Only a few better-off families in the village were to prepare meals for however many activists in hiding there were on a given day. And the women doing this were asked to leave the cooked food in their kitchen.

'They did not know who it was who came and picked up the food. Nor did they know who the individuals were that they were cooking for. The resistance never used people from the village to do the transportation. The British had spies and informants in the village. So did the feudal zamindars who were their collaborators. These informants would recognize locals carrying loads to the forest. That would endanger both the women and the underground. Nor could they have anyone identifying the people they sent in—probably by nightfall—to collect the food. The women never saw who it was lifting the meals.

'That way, both were shielded from exposure. But the women knew what was going on. Most village women would gather each morning at the ponds and streams, tanks—and those involved exchanged notes and experiences. They knew why and what they were doing it for—but never specifically for whom.'

The 'women' included young girls barely in their teens. All of them risking very serious consequences. What if the police landed up at Bhabani's house? What would become of her and the family that depended on her, as she points out, for 'everything'? Largely, though, the underground protocols worked.

Yet, families embracing *swadeshi*, the *charkha* and other symbols of resistance to the British were always under surveillance. The dangers were real.

So what did Bhabani cook for those in hiding? She has Partha *da* explain it to us after our meeting. *Jonar* (maize), *kodo* (ditch millet or Indian cow grass), *madwa* (*ragi* or finger millet) and any vegetables the women could get. Which means, thanks to Bhabani and her friends, they could often consume the same staples they had at home.

On some occasions, they had puffed or flattened rice—*chinre* (*poha*) in Bengali. The women sometimes also sent them fruit. Besides which they would eat wild fruit and berries. One item the old-timers recall is *kyand* (or *tiril*). In more than one tribal language, that simply means 'fruit of the forest'.

Partha *da* says his grandad, as a young husband, would suddenly show up and place orders with Bhabani. When this was for friends in the forest, it inevitably meant preparing food for many more people.

And it wasn't just the British who were a problem. In the 1940s, her load was heaviest during the years of the Great Bengal Famine. The hardships she must have endured in that period defy the imagination.

So, looking back, what does she think of Gandhi, ahimsa, and satyagraha now? While she is outspoken and to the point on most things, she finds questions she sees as larger philosophical ones confusing. What is clear is that she was and remains idealistic on her own plane. That she knew what she was doing—risking her life—in aiding the resistance to the Raj.

Her adventures continued after Independence. These too, were marked by idealism and caring for others. In the 1950s, a huge fire razed the entire *mohallah* or neighbourhood where the family still lives. It destroyed all stocks of grain held by people there. Bhabani brought in grain and produce from her own family's lands in the village of Janra. And sustained the entire community for weeks till the next harvest.

In 1964, a major communal flare-up rocked nearby Jamshedpur in what was then Bihar. Its flames scorched some villages in Puruliya as well. Bhabani sheltered many Muslims of her village in her own house.

Two decades later, an already ageing Bhabani killed a wild cat that was raiding the livestock of the locals. She did that, says Partha *da*, with a stout piece of wood. It turned out to be a *khatas*, or small Indian civet, coming out of the forest.

We look at Bhabani Mahato with renewed respect. I remembered the story I had done on freedom fighter Ganpati Yadav. A courier of the underground in Satara, he carried food into the forests for the fighters hiding out there. He was still cycling 90 kilometres a day at 98 when I met him. I loved doing that story on the wonderful man. But had failed to ask him: he carried so much food into the forests at great risk, but what about his wife who did the cooking?

She was away with relatives when I visited him.

Ganpati has passed, but our encounter with Bhabani makes me realize one thing: I need to go back and speak to Vatsala Ganpati Yadav. And have her tell her own story.

Bhabani also makes me recall those powerful words of Laxmi Panda, the Odia freedom fighter who had joined Netaji Bose's Indian National Army and had been in their camps, both in the forests of Burma (now Myanmar) and in Singapore.

'Because I never went to jail, because I trained with a rifle but never fired a bullet at anyone, does that mean I am not a freedom fighter? I only worked in INA forest camps that were targets of British bombing. Does that mean I made no contribution to the freedom struggle? At 13, I was cooking in the camp kitchens for all those who were going out and fighting, was I not part of that?'

Bhabani, like Laxmi Panda, Salihan, Hausabai Patil and Vatsala Yadav, never received the honours and recognition she truly deserved. In the struggle for India's freedom, all of them fought and acquitted themselves as honourably as anyone else. But they were women. In societies awash in prejudices and stereotypes against women, their role was seldom valued.

This doesn't seem to bother Bhabani Mahato, though. Perhaps she has internalized those values? Perhaps it leads her to undervalue her own unique contribution?

But the last thing she tells us as we leave is this: 'Look at what I nurtured. This large family, all these generations, our farm, everything. But these younger people . . .' Several granddaughters-in-law seem to be working around us with the greatest diligence. They are obviously doing their best. Yet, it's what she did single-handedly in her time.

She isn't blaming them or anyone else, really. She just regrets there are fewer people who can do 'everything'.

Scan QR code for PARI Freedom Fighters Gallery.

14

H. S. DORESWAMY

ONE NEWSPAPER, MANY NAMES

'The Collector did not enquire why I was registering so many newspapers. The point is, when they shut down one title, I could re-launch under another. So when they shut down *Pauravani*, I started *Pauraveera*.'

—H. S. Doreswamy, Bengaluru, Karnataka

'I shifted the newspaper *Pauravani* to Hindupur, which was then in Anantapur district of Madras Presidency. That was to get around the shutdown of the paper in what was then the Mysore princely state. I went to the Collector of Anantapur district to get the paper registered. There, I declared myself to be the editor of *Pauravani* [Citizen's Voice]. Also of *Pauraveera*, *Paurabhaskara* and *Pauramartanda*, all newspapers in the Kannada language.

'The Collector did not enquire why I was registering so many newspapers. The point is, when they shut down one title, I could re-launch under another. So when they shut down *Pauravani*, I started *Pauraveera* [Citizen's Champion]. That lasted some thirty-eight days. About the duration of the peak period of the *Mysore Chalo* movement in 1947.

'Yes, it was still 1947, and the paper's closure and my arrest were imminent. That's why I shifted to Hindupur, which bordered the Mysore state. We were at the time campaigning for the *Mysore Chalo* movement.' That was a people's movement demanding the integration of the princely state into a newly emerging India. The new *Pauraveera* had the same content, same writers and staff as the suppressed *Pauravani*.

That was one among many diverse tactics used by Indian journalists and newspapers during the freedom struggle. The classic one being, of course, the *Amrita Bazar Patrika* in Bengal converting itself into an English publication overnight in 1878. The British had brought in the Vernacular Press Act that year. The new Act aimed at curbing criticism of the Raj in the Indian language newspapers. So the *Patrika* switched from Bengali to English, which had been excluded from the law's ambit.

Over six decades later, Harohalli Srinivasaiah Doreswamy would not switch languages. Just newspaper titles.

So that's what he was in the 1930s and 1940s—a seasoned journalist?

'I didn't know anything about it,' he scoffs. 'I was not a journalist. I was forced to take it up because of the appeal of my predecessor Rumale Bhadranna, a dear friend. He died of hydrophobia caused by dog bite. When he was about to expire, all of us—his friends—assembled by his bedside. He said with folded hands, "The paper will have to continue. Some of you will have to take it up and do it."

'I had to do it,' he says.

And how.

In his 104th year, veteran freedom fighter H. S. Doreswamy remains an active writer and author. He still publishes journalistic pieces now and then. And that's almost seven decades after keeping that single newspaper of many titles going for years. 'Back in those days, I was publisher and seller,' he laughs. Also, part-time printer, manager and one of the writers.

The old Gandhian is talking to us at his residence in Bengaluru in March 2021. He's propped up in a bed—recovering from the prolonged effects of COVID-19. But his mind, clarity and wit remain sharp as ever.

The once-reluctant journalist went on to be a founder member of the Mysore Journalists Union. And later of the Karnataka unit of the Indian Federation of Working Journalists (KFWJ).

After India attained Independence, he started a publishing house called Sahitya Mandira that lasted for decades. It also had a bookstore in Bengaluru that the famous writer R. K. Narayan visited more than once. But even prior to 1947, he would publish and sell booklets, books and political tracts. From the late 1940s onwards, he made a living off it.

Doreswamy at his home in Jayanagar, March 2021. He had been ill, but still remained active. He still took part in online events.

'Three books a year,' he says is 'what I brought out.' His mind is now moving between periods pre- and post-1947. 'If I got thirty rupees a month, I would eat *roti* and porridge. If I got three hundred rupees, I would have a feast. We sold the books for about five to ten rupees each. Prior to 1947, we sold *Pauravani* for three paise a copy.' He has no number for how many pieces or books he's actually written. He never bothered to count.

In 2018, at age 100, the man who 'didn't know anything about' journalism was awarded the Basava Puraskara for, among other things, journalism. That's a state award in Karnataka given to the most distinguished individuals across diverse fields. Among past winners: former President of India A. P. J. Abdul Kalam for the year 2006. Doreswamy won it for his contribution to journalism, the freedom struggle and social work.

'Once, when we were in prison in Bengaluru (1942–43), it was midnight, and a group of captives was brought in. They came in shouting slogans, and we thought they were more of our people. But they weren't. They were Indian military personnel. We were told they were officers but didn't know for sure. We didn't know their ranks.

'There were fourteen of them—from different states. They had decided to leave the British Indian military and join Netaji Bose's Indian National Army (INA). They tried to leave the country. And were on their way to Burma [now Myanmar] when they were arrested. All fourteen of them. They were brought to Bengaluru and court-martialled. And sentenced to death by hanging.

'We interacted with them. They wrote down, with their blood, a letter to all of us. It said, "We are so happy that you are 500 here. This country, this Bharat Mata, requires the blood of so many people. We are also a part and parcel of that effort. We have also pledged to give our lives to this country's cause." That is what they wrote.

'The next day, when the jail superintendent came, they were produced before him. The Englishman who had brought them, also a military officer I think, spoke to the superintendent. He told him you should hang all these people and give me possession of the bodies. He demanded they be hanged simultaneously.

'The superintendent—his name was Latif—replied that the jail manuals and protocols did not permit that. Not more than two people could be hanged at one time. The English officer said he could give at most seven days for the hangings to be done and the bodies handed over. The jail officials did not agree.

'In the night again we heard the slogans of these Indian officers. They were being taken back to Jalahalli, to a British military base. [Jalahalli is today an Indian Air Force base.]

'We heard that all of them were lined up in a row and shot dead—*all* of them—at one time.' He's silent a few moments after that.

Then: 'They knew it. That they were going to their death. But they were very cheerful. That's why they gave us that letter written in blood addressed to all of us.'

But how did Doreswamy find his way to prison in the first place? Was it just the textile workers' strike of 1942 that he had aided and abetted? Or something to do with bombs going off in post boxes and government record offices?

'There was this thing nicknamed "time bomb",' he smiles. 'It was quite harmless. A small item we had to put into the post box. Once inside, it would go off after some ten minutes. It would burn all the letters and things in the box. We only did this in post boxes located at government offices [and record rooms].

'So it would disrupt government correspondence and communications. It wouldn't explode. It would just catch fire. There was no explosion at all.'

But where did Doreswamy get this device or the material for it?

'There was one Mr Bhuja Das. He was a graduate. He was preparing it in his godowns and supplying it to me. He used to give it to others as well, in other districts.

'I had supplied this material to one K. Ramachandra from Tumkur. He got caught and was brought to Bangalore [now Bengaluru]. At midnight, the police came and searched my house. They found nothing. I was more concerned that it would be my elder brother who would be arrested. He was more active than me at that time.

(That elder brother, H. S. Sitaram, would one day be the Mayor of Bangalore in free India.)

'But the police just held me. They said, "One Ramachandra has come, and he says you have given him bombs. We have caught him red-handed, and he is now in our custody. You please come with us now to the station."

'So I went to the police station with them. There, he was brought before me. The police surrounded us with lathis and put me in the middle. I thought I'd die if any one of them beat me even once. As a matter of fact,' he laughs, 'that became a common experience for me later! At that moment, though, I even perspired.

'Ultimately, I took courage. And when Ramachandra said I had supplied it, I replied, "I have not given you this thing." I said I was in Shimoga [now officially known as Shivamogga] at the time. I was there with the conservator of forests, and I can bring him as a witness.

'Finally, the police took him to the court for enquiry. To me, they said, "We have no proof of what you did. But we want to prevent you acting during the movement." [This was in the continuing disquiet of the Quit India stir.] And so they put me in jail for twelve months. Without any enquiry.'

Born on 10 April 1918, Doreswamy was just 24 at the time of his jailing.

'They did produce me before the court. Where they said because he (that is, me) is a potential troublemaker, we need to hold him for a long time.

'When I came out, the movement had died down. One by one, all the leaders of the country, who were in jail, were being released at that time.'

Prior to his foray into journalism, Doreswamy was briefly a teacher. 'I completed primary school in my native village Harohalli [today in Ramanagar district of Karnataka]. Then I came to Bengaluru, where I completed my schooling. I then took a BSc degree from Central College here.

'I was a teacher in the Gandhinagar Higher Secondary School for six months. That is from June to December 1942. I severed my ties with the school in December as I was arrested [for the first of many times in his life].'

Doreswamy collaborated with 'Communist leader N. D. Shankar in shutting down the three textile mills—Binny, Raja and Minerva—for fourteen days'. There had been earlier strikes too, in the mills, he says. But coming when it did, it added heft to the anti-British feeling, he feels. And so this shutdown angered the government more.

'We had formed the "Ginger Group" within the Congress Party quite early in Mysore. We all wanted Independence and unification to happen early.'

'Ginger Group'? Does he mean the Congress Socialist Party, that group within the Congress?

'Yes. We used to call it the Ginger Group here. We were trying to influence the Congress from within. There were many of us. One Mrs Seetharamaiah was there. Also, S. S. Shastry, K. S. Kumaran, Shridhar. And so many others. Even when that great moment arrived in 1947, we were there. The paper *Pauravani* was there to campaign. Simply, we wanted to call for early action so we could get a democratic government sooner. In Mysore state, as in India.

'When the Britishers left the country, they did so with three formulae. One, to form Pakistan and Hindustan. Two, to keep the people in both countries divided on communal lines. And three: those 562 princely states—they were free to join or stay out of this Indian Union.

'The Maharaja of Mysore was by himself a very good man. A statesman, even. But with all that, he was still beholden to the British. He was always obedient to them.* So he did not want to join this union.

'At that time my paper [*Pauravani*] was there. I went on writing. Also, there was one T. T. Sharman. He was editor of *Vishwa Karnataka*. He wrote around eight articles about the Maharaja, about the state of Mysore. We printed all the articles one by one in *Pauravani*. By the time we put out the sixth piece, we got a notice from the Chief Secretary of Mysore.

'It said that if thereafter we were to publish any articles or editorials on the subject, we would have to submit them to the government. That is prior to publication. Simply: pre-censorship. Only what the government admitted to or agreed with could be published by us. I did not care for that pre-censorship.

'I had two more of those pieces still with me. We published them. I ran a box with the articles declaring we would not bow down to the dictators of this government. That we would close

---

* T. R. Sathish Kumar, 'A throwback to Mysore Chalo', *Deccan Herald,* 14 August 2021, available at https://www.deccanherald.com/spectrum/spectrum-statescan/a-throwback-to-mysore-chalo-1019703.html, accessed on 4 September 2022.

the paper in protest. The next day I was told that the paper's office had been locked. And that I was to be arrested.'

It was time to shift *Pauravani* to Hindupur in Madras Presidency. The rest is history.

For the next three decades almost, he worked as a writer, author and publisher.

Doreswamy shut down *Pauravani* after 1947. He felt, says his son D. Raju, who is 70, 'that it had served its purpose. Independence had been achieved'.

'I was arrested in 1975, during the Emergency. For what? For writing a letter to Prime Minister Indira Gandhi.

'I wrote to her saying—you are ruling in the name of a democracy. But you are acting like a dictator. And you have threatened newspapers. You don't like it when people mention the place and conditions under which prisoners are kept and all. This is very horrible. If you continue like this, I shall go around the country, around the villages and tell people you are a dictator.

'I then held a meeting at Tagore Circle in Basavanagudi. And I was arrested.'

Surely that caused problems for his family?

'Of course. My son Raju—he is a BSc BE—ran into trouble. He was studying in his final year at an engineering college [The University BDT College of Engineering, Davangere]. My son wrote to my wife, saying I had not paid his hostel fees for two months. If I didn't pay for one more month, he would be turned out of the hostel. She in turn told me about it.

'I told her I was helpless. I could do nothing in this matter. That too, while in jail. Ask him to come back home, I told her. He can attend the final examinations next year. Or if he so desires, let him come to jail. Let him have the experience of jail.

'But, in the meantime, some of my friends got to learn of this. They went to my home and spoke to my wife Lalithamma. They enquired about any troubles she was facing. She said she had none herself, but that our son was stranded in his college. If he was unable to pay the fees any longer, he would have to vacate the hostel. Our friends took it up as their duty to resolve the problem. And they went there and paid all the pending dues.

'They also told my son: If after two months, your father is still not released, you should write to us. We will respond at once. But at no time should you consider giving up on your studies.'

Meanwhile, 'after being detained for four months, my case came before the Magistrate. He criticized the police. I had been held under the Defence of India Rules, 1962 (DIR). He told them I was "not an enemy of India". And that I had every right to criticize my Prime Minister. So I am going to release him. Ask the government, he told the prosecutor, what other sections they have under which he can be punished.'

For a person of Doreswamy's erudition, intellect and talents, why did he exist on the borderline of poverty for decades?

'The volume *My Early Life* by Gandhiji was my life's textbook. There he had written that a social worker should embrace voluntary poverty. Somehow that idea caught my imagination. The significance of it came to me later when I had to face familial life. I knew I should be content with what I have. If I want to be a full-time worker, then I would have to live by doing something on my own.

'That was when I decided to publish books, two or three a year. I would go to colleges and talk to them about Gandhi and other things. Then ask them if they were going to buy the books. They gladly purchased those.'

That was how his publishing outfit Sahitya Mandir began on a regular basis in 1950. It was also the year he got married—'at age 32'. To a lady 'who a friend of mine was giving tuitions to. We got married and we had two children, a son and a daughter'.

The son, D. Raju, now 70, and his wife Chandrika Raju, who is 62, live just a kilometre away from Doreswamy's home in Jayanagar in the city. His daughter, Veena Venkateshmurthy, who is also 62, lives in Bengaluru's J. P. Nagar locality.

'Back in 1950, when I got married, I was into Vinobha Bhave's Bhoodan movement and out twenty-four days in a month. We stayed in a rented home. All I was getting was Rs 100 a month from the Gandhi Fund (before Sahitya Mandir started earning its way). I used to give her that.

'My wife ran everything. Looked after the children, everything. All of it happened because of her effort and support.'

She had no objections to his running around as an activist?

'She might have had, but she never gave me a hard time over it. She always cooperated.'

Lalithamma died in 2019, in her eighty-ninth year.

Doreswamy 'is a fake freedom fighter'. Also, 'an anti-national'. And 'a Pakistani agent'.*

Those were just a few of the many abuses hurled at the old fighter in early 2020. They came from Bharatiya Janata Party (BJP) leaders in Karnataka. They included an MLA who was a former Minister. Among other things, his attackers claimed, he had never been a part of the struggle. His jail record was 'a fake'. They demanded that his freedom fighter's pension, which he was getting since 1972, be withdrawn.

It did not matter that proof of his jail time existed. *The Indian Express* even published a certificate signed by a superintendent of the Central Jail Bangalore in 1971 to that effect. The certificate is clear about his status as a prisoner there.

---

* 'Yatnal calls Doreswamy 'fake freedom fighter', 'Pak. agent', *The Hindu*, 25 February 2020, available at https://www.thehindu.com/news/national/karnataka/yatnal-calls-doreswamy-fake-freedom-fighter-pak-agent/article30915710.ece, accessed on 4 September 2022.

Responding to attacks on his freedom fighter credentials,
Doreswamy's admirers brought out this booklet:
'A *Gandhivaadi* replies to *Godsevaadis*'.

'He was admitted into this jail on 18.12.1942 and was released
on 8.12.1943 . . .' it says.

Then why the barrage of invective and falsehoods?

In the eyes of the ruling BJP, Doreswamy had committed the ultimate crime. He had criticized Prime Minister Narendra Modi. He had openly voiced his support for the ongoing anti-Citizenship (Amendment) Act (CAA) stir across the country. He had even appeared on a public stage, at age 102, with the protestors to condemn the CAA.

His attackers took no note of the fact that he had also once written a strong letter to a Congress Prime Minister. One that had landed him in jail for four months. Nor did they care that 'as a citizen I have the right to criticize my Prime Minister'.

'I am writing my CV now,' he told the *Express*, with characteristic wry humour. To prove his credentials, as it were.

At his home in March 2021, he showed us a response to the attacks. A booklet brought out by his admirers titled 'A *Gandhivaadi* replies to *Godsevaadis*'. That is, a pupil of Gandhi replies to the followers of Nathuram Godse, who assassinated him.

'His last book—and he had more than he could count—was a wonderful one on the Sarvodaya movement,' says his son, D. Raju. 'He gave me the proofs just six months before his demise. And he handed over that volume to the Gandhi Bhavan in Bengaluru.'

Doreswamy's last column appeared in the weekly *Nyaya Patha* of 12 May 2021. Just two weeks before his demise of cardiac arrest on 26 May that year. The piece analyses the Assembly poll results in Tamil Nadu, West Bengal and Kerala that were out barely ten days earlier.

The column has him yet again asserting his right to criticize his Prime Minister. He is also scathing about sycophantic television channels that gloss over his 'failure in every step in the fight against corona'. He notes the rout of the BJP in those three states. Yet, has this to say to that party: 'Democracy is not just about winning elections. It is more important to find proper solutions to the challenges facing society.'

Scan QR code for PARI Freedom Fighters Gallery.

15

THELU AND LOKKHI MAHATO

BETWEEN BAPU AND THE BANDITS

'My father and his forefathers—they were forced to grow indigo by the British. Our parents and grandparents could not resist the British might.'

—Thelu Mahato, Puruliya, West Bengal

'There were around 1,500 of us gathered to gherao the police station in Manbazar. We were sick and tired of the torment and torture of British rule. Besides, there had been recent attacks by their agents, the feudal Raja's goondas, on our villages. People were very distressed.

'The call had gone out as part of the Quit India agitation, and people began marching on twelve police stations in Puruliya from 29 September 1942. The next day saw them converge at those stations. I was with the crowd in Manbazar. Some of our leaders intended to raise the national flag atop the station. A few protestors climbed the roof of the building and started removing its terracotta tiles.

'The British police opened fire and two people died. Chunaram Mahato died on the spot. Gobinda Mahato died in the hospital. They were the ones trying to raise the flag. They were unarmed and were gunned down in front of our eyes. Girish Mahato was hit by a bullet that lodged in his body.

'The police fired recklessly into the crowd as well. That's when a gherao turned into an attack on the station. People thought those two—Chunaram and Gobinda—might still be alive and were being held captive. And our intent was to free them. Some others, like Tularam Mahato, died later in British jails.

'Magaram Mahato and Baidyanath Mahato, both organizers of the protest, had been to jail before. They were hunted down again and thrown into Baghalpur Jail [now in Bihar],' says Thelu. 'There were seven of us from my village in the action that day in 1942. At age 105 today, I am the only survivor from that group.'

Thelu Mahato is gentle, self-effacing, bright-eyed and alert. He is surely the oldest survivor of the police station attack. And maybe the oldest freedom fighter still alive in Puruliya (also spelt Purulia) district and all of West Bengal. He is, as we later learnt, somewhere between 102 and 105 years old.

Thelu—meaning 'one who pushes'—got his name from a Brahmin *purohit*. The priest tagged him with it because he was born at the fag end of his father's funeral rites. In other words, he had pushed his father away from this world.

Seated beside him is his lifelong friend Lokkhikanto Mahato, aged 97. 'Lokkhi' was not part of the events of

30 September 1942 at the police station. He was probably just a tad under the age limit of 17 set by the leaders of the agitation for participation in the gherao.

In any case, Lokkhi was far more involved in the cultural side of the resistance. He was part of troupes that performed on tribal instruments such as *dhamsa* (a large kettle drum) and *madol* (a hand drum). These were commonly used by Santhals, Kurmis, Birhors and other Adivasi groups. Lokkhi's troupes also sang what at one level seemed to be innocuous folk songs.

In the context of that time, however, these songs took on a different meaning. The drum-beating messengers and singers also spread the message of rebellion against British rule. Lokkhi is still a handsome man of impressive bearing. With a visage that at once reminds you of Rabindranath Tagore. And a clear, resonant voice for a singer aged 97.

'We also used to shout *Vande Mataram* now and then,' says Lokkhi. They had no real affinity for the cry or the song. 'But it angered the British,' he says, smiling.

'It was all chaos,' resumes Thelu about 30 September. 'We took Girish Mahato to a doctor. His name, I think, was Dr Annindo, and he was pro-British. "You deserve it," he told us and refused to help. So we took Girish to another doctor—and there were not so many in those days. But we found one to help extract the bullet.' However, Girish too would soon be captured and sent to Bhagalpur Jail.

'Meanwhile, in the crackdown that followed, many of us fled into the forests and went into hiding.'

But hold on, we ask. This was part of the August Quit India agitation? In end-September 1942?

'Yes,' says Thelu smiling. 'It took a long time in those days for news from outside to reach these parts. We got to know only a month after 8 August of the Mahatma's call. And all different groups took time to come together, organize and act.'

They are speaking to us on 26 March 2022, at Thelu's dismal one-room semi-pukka home in Pirra village of Puncha block in West Bengal's Puruliya district. Almost eighty years after the march on the police stations. Both have been denied freedom fighter's pensions. And have long ago given up on trying to get those. Thelu lives on a 1,000-rupee old-age pension. Lokkhi received his old-age pension for all of one month. Then it mysteriously stopped.

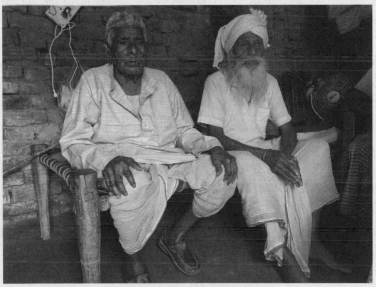

Thelu Mahato and Lokkhi Mahato at Thelu's one-room home in Pirra village, Puruliya district, West Bengal, in March 2022.

Thelu and Lokkhi are keen, even anxious, to tell their story. They want newer generations to know that they stood up for their country and are proud of having done so.

Bipin Sardar, Digambar Sardar and Pitambar Sardar. Three dacoits and bandits revered by Thelu and Lokkhi, who had a profound impact on both in their formative years. All three were from the Bhumij tribal community.

'They stole from the rich landlords and gave a lot to the poor peasants and labourers,' says Thelu. 'Digam and Pitam Sardar were brothers from Kusumdihi village. Bipin Sardar was from Dihagora village.

'The feudal landlords lived in terror of these three. But poor people revered them as "Gurudev". You have to understand what a terrible feudal society existed here. The Raja—Karuna Sindhu Patar—ran the cruellest regime you could imagine. His family, also of the Bhumij community, had control of hundreds of *bighas* of land. They collected taxes for the British. Apart from their own thugs, the police often camped at their house.'

The Raja, Lokkhi says, 'would order five to six villages to come with their ploughs [on a given day] to his place. And order them to "prepare my land for cultivation this season". They were paid nothing, it was *begari* [forced labour]. All they got was a few fistfuls of broken, flattened rice. This outrage was repeated at harvest time'.

Both he and Thelu say that no matter how bad things are today, they were worse then. The British police and the feudal thugs would very often beat up people. 'They would grab our valuables and livestock. Often, they set fire to our huts and *morais* [traditional silos for unthreshed paddy]. They would even set ablaze *gowals* [cattle-sheds],' they recall.

'*Lal topi dikhlei dor lagto* [We would shiver at the sight of the red turbans—of the police and Raja's thugs],' says Lokkhi.

There is one story from that feudal era that we do not discuss. Any mention of it has Thelu go silent and deeply emotional. We learn that he got married before he was 25 to a very pretty young woman. But a local landlord from his own Kurmi community forcibly abducted his wife and mother-in-law. A helpless Thelu never fully got over that. He never remarried. He threw himself into working on his family's eight to ten bighas (or about two to two-and-a-half acres) of land. And looking after his two brothers and their children.

All he will confirm about that tragedy is: 'No, I never saw them [wife and mother-in-law] ever again.'

In that universe, Bipin, Digambar and Pitambar Sardar were the Robin Hoods of Puruliya. Outlaws whom people turned to for justice.

The stories Thelu and Lokkhi narrate about them reminds us of historian Eric Hobsbawm's brilliant 1969 book, *Bandits*. In it, Hobsbawm looks at the bandit phenomenon in many countries, including India. He views it across Europe, Asia, Africa and Latin America. He speaks of 'social banditry' that can be brutal, violent and terrifying. But which at the same time 'simultaneously challenges the economic and social political order'. And does so 'by challenging those who hold or lay claim to power, law and the control of resources'.

Thirty years later, Hobsbawm revised the book. Because he felt the need to emphasize more strongly, 'the *political history* of the role of banditry . . . (as) central'.

Bipin and Digambar were once caught by the British and were to be deported to the Andamans, say Thelu and Lokkhi. 'But while they were crossing the river here, a young British officer fell overboard. Digambar jumped in and rescued him. For all we know, it was Bipin and Digambar who pushed him into the water. But impressed by Digambar's bravery, the authorities reduced their sentence. They were spared the Andamans and sent to Puruliya's old jail instead.

'From there, they escaped on a rainy night. They jumped into the Kangsabati river and swam to a rock formation in Borahantu hamlet near Kaira village, not far from Pirra. They formed a new base in a network of caves there and resumed their banditry. Just before 1947, all three were arrested again and died while in prison.'

Thelu actually met Bipin Sardar when the bandit was already an old man. His attitude towards the trio seems to be an odd mix of revulsion and reverence. Lokkhi broadly shares this perspective. Both understood the place of the bandits in feudal Puruliya. They realized their societal relevance. But they also were attracted by Gandhi's teachings of ahimsa or non-violence.

So how do Thelu and Lokkhi, staunch Leftists all their lives, reconcile all this with their Gandhian norms? And with admiration for the bandits? And with supporting the attack on the Manbazar police station?

'Look,' says Thelu, 'they opened fire on us. Of course, people would retaliate when they saw their friends, family or comrades shot by police before their eyes.'

As they speak, we realize once more that we are running into a major strand of the freedom struggle. Yet again.

Thelu and Lokkhi Mahato were and are Leftist by persuasion and Gandhian by personality. Leftist by passion and politics. Gandhian by moral code and lifestyle. Closer home, their hero was Netaji Bose. Gandhi was more distant, but a towering figure they held in awe. I was to think of them again when, barely three weeks later, I would meet Shobharam Gehervar, the fascinating freedom fighter of Ajmer (see Chapter 4).

Shobharam is a Dalit and self-declared Gandhian. He also deeply admires Dr Ambedkar. He told me this: 'I was with both, *Gandhivad* and *krantivad* [Gandhian path and revolutionary movement]. Both were closely linked.' So, while primarily a Gandhian, there were three political streams he associated with.

Thelu and Lokkhi tell me that 'every home in our younger days had a *charkha*. Mostly the women were in charge of that spinning'. That generation 'also boycotted clothes from Manchester and other British goods', says Partha Sarathi Mahato, a schoolteacher. His grandfather Baidyanath was one of the organizers of the 30 September 1942 action.

The shaping of the Puruliya duo also had much to do with where they came from. The society around them.

Both Thelu and Lokkhi Mahato are Kurmis, the largest community in West Bengal's Jangalmahal region. The Kurmis were amongst the earliest to rise against the East India Company—alongside the Bhumij and other tribes of the region in the 1760s. The British dubbed the Bhumijas and their allies as 'Chuars', and the series of revolts here as the 'Chuar Rebellion', a derogatory term history books still repeat. In Bengali, 'Chuar' means 'uncivilized' or 'barbaric'.

It was, in fact, a genuine struggle of the oppressed. And one of the earliest fights for freedom from the British. The Adivasis of Jangalmahal and surrounding areas kept that rebellion going for over four decades.

The Kurmis were robbed of tribal status by the British. The Raj did list them as a Scheduled Tribe in 1913. But dropped them from that group in the 1931 Census. Perhaps as a punishment for their rebellious attitude.

In India of the 1950s, they were, oddly, listed as OBCs. Restoration of their tribal status remains a major demand of Kurmis in this state. All the older Kurmis we speak to—not just Thelu and Lokkhi—still feel that, at their core, they are a tribe.

Kurmis were also at the forefront of the freedom struggle in Puruliya. Scores of them took part in the march on the twelve police stations in the last two days of September 1942. Thelu and Lokkhi fought many battles thereafter too. All the way to Independence and beyond.

Barely a day before 15 August 1947, Thelu says, 'I was tending to our buffaloes in the fields near Pirra. Suddenly, there were villagers yelling: "The British *saabs* are running away in military vehicles filled with gold, precious metals and other wealth." And crowds began to collect.

'But celebrations, too, began. Magaram Mahato's family held a feast that fed our entire village.'

Both Thelu and Lokkhi are remarkably fit for their advanced age. Each walks about 4–5 kilometres every day within the village of Pirra. The thin coloured cloth Thelu is wearing over his shoulder is a *'gamcha'*.

I hear Tusu is going south
What is she going to eat if hungry?
*Bring me Tusu's gamcha**
I will pack some sweets made of ghee.

That's 97-year-old Lokkhi singing for us. Well, at least, that's what we figure his age is—six to eight years younger than Thelu. Going by their Aadhaar cards, Thelu is 97 and Lokkhi, 89. Both protest this vehemently.

Documenting the age of poor people in remote rural regions is tricky at the best of times. In the era they were born in, it was almost non-existent. Neither has any reason to lie about his age. Nor anything to gain from doing so. We checked with their families, with younger contemporaries who were witness to the Manbazar and other events. And with families of other (now deceased) freedom fighters—like that of Baidyanath Mahato.

This led us to conclude that Thelu is somewhere between 102 and 105 and Lokkhi around 97. This is, at any rate, a more reliable reckoning than the arbitrary ages handed out to people of that generation by the dysfunctional Aadhaar card system here.

But when they found this was wrong, we ask, why did they not contest it with the Aadhaar authorities? Lokkhi scoffs: 'We were told that it would be a troublesome process.

---

* A traditional thin, coarse cotton cloth, used as a towel, a scarf or even a turban. The *gamcha* is also famous as a saratorial symbol with innovative designs and adaptive qualities.

That it might up end up with them introducing more mistakes on our cards.'

Oh, well, maybe he could give us another song instead? Surely, a more pleasurable act than exploring the bureaucratic absurdities of Aadhaar. Lokkhi is a bit shy. But he obliges:

> *I used to visit your home*
> *As Tusu was residing there*
> *Now that Tusu is gone*
> *I have no business at your home.*

This genre of song is called Tusu *gaan*, linked to the Tusu or harvest festival of Kurmis. Tusu is more a secular festival. Not a religious one. These were songs once sung only by unmarried girls, but which developed a following beyond that group. In the songs Lokkhi sings, Tusu is seen as a young female spirit. The second of the songs seems to mark the end of the festival.

So what did they harvest here—and what did they mainly consume? Rice, as might be expected in West Bengal? No, say both Thelu and Lokkhi.

'*Boda log bhat khato* [the rich ate rice],' says Lokkhi. 'We mainly ate millets.'

That is certainly a surprise. But, they explain: 'The Raja and the landlords, they ate rice. And even then, there was some processing of it. We had good local varieties of rice. But more and more, it started coming from outside.'

'Rice loses nourishment in pounding and boiling. Millets were more nutritious,' says Thelu. But millets, including ragi, lost ground as rice emerged as a status symbol. Also, it fetched a better price for farmers than millet. And the process quickened with rice and wheat ruling the public distribution system that came in after Independence. 'Besides,' says Sishir Kumar Mahato, a grand-nephew of freedom fighter Magaram Mahato, 'local varieties were not considered high yielding. So rice caught on.'

'Mostly, before that, it was maize, *ragi, kado* [kodo millet],' says Thelu. 'Paddy came much later.'

'We consumed milk, *jonar* [maize] and millet,' says Lokkhi. 'Rice was for rare or festive occasions. We also ate local fruits we collected by hand in and around the forests.'

Thelu explains to us that their agriculture here was for long, pesticide-free. Also, chemical fertilizer-free. The many decades he spent working on the fields have given him deep insights into cultivation and crops. He gives us a concise history of farming in the region in the past 200 years.

Everything Thelu and Lokkhi need, they do or create themselves. Given their advanced age, they are in remarkable shape. Both draw their own bathing water from a well, wash their own clothes and walk 4–5 kilometres within the village every day.

A well he dug in his courtyard, all by himself, is what Thelu is most proud of. He insists on showing us the well and wants to be photographed beside it. There are multiple little dwellings he built on his land—with his own hands. These are now occupied by his nephews and grand-nephews—to whom he signed off all his lands a day or two before we meet him.

He lives by himself in that tin-roofed room. One that was allotted to him by the last Left Front government before 2011. His one joy is spending time with his neighbours—Amol, Shubhankar and Maumita Mahato, who deeply respect and care for him. 'We love feeding *Dadu*,' says Maumita—as she gives all of us lunch. Earlier, she had told my colleague Smita Khator: 'It was one of the things that brightened the news of my marriage to Shubhankar being fixed. That I would be living next door to a freedom fighter.'

Puruliya remains West Bengal's poorest district. Young people from here, we learn, migrate in large numbers to other districts in the state such as Bardhaman. And to Maharashtra, Kerala and other states, where they work as farm labourers and construction workers.

Like Bhabani Mahato (see Chapter 13) in Chepua village of the Manbazar 1 block, neither Thelu nor Lokkhi conform to stereotypes of what a freedom fighter should be like. Certainly not those created by state and elite society. Nor are they unidimensional people who just made up the numbers at protests. Both speak knowledgeably on their subjects. Lokkhi on music and culture. Thelu on farming and the region's history.

'My father and his forefathers—they were forced to grow indigo by the British,' says Thelu. It's the first time I learn that Puruliya was part of the indigo belt stretching outward from Champaran in Bihar. 'Our parents and grandparents could not resist the British might.'

'We worked on the land at the pleasure of the Raja,' says Thelu. 'We had no deed, no record of these eight to ten *bighas* being cultivated by us.' That only came after 1978, with 'Operation Barga' carried out by the then Left Front government. They had good relations with that government, but remained independent of it. And took part in protests against it when they felt they had good reason to.

The two of them used to walk 40 kilometres to the market with their harvested produce before 1947. That could weigh as much as 60 kilograms. But why walk?

There was no such thing as public transport in those days. 'The coming of the cycle was a huge thing here,' says Thelu. 'But none of us could ever afford one. A few times we saw Raja Karuna Sindhu Patar on a cycle, we would say: "Look, he is flying."'

As we leave Pirra, we drop in at the home of 96-year-old Banalata Mahato in Matyala village of Manbazar 1 block. Her husband was the Girish Mahato, who was wounded at the Manbazar police station in 1942. Girish died in 2002 or 2003.

Like Bhabani Mahato, she plays down her own role in the freedom struggle. But she is aware and proud of it. Through the periods when Girish was on the run, she was 'feeding and caring for him and his fellow fugitives'. She was also organizing help for many in the neighbourhood. 'Girish went to Bhagalpur Jail for some years,' she says. She worked behind the scenes in aiding the resistance. 'I always followed Gandhiji's ahimsa,' she tells us.

Many others from their village had also been jailed. Banalata 'gathered the neighbours and ran everything to assist all people here'. She remained active after 1947. It's only from others we learn that 'Banalata once walked from here in Puruliya to Kolkata on foot' during a protest in the 1950s. That's a distance of over 270 kilometres today. It might have been more in that era.

In little-written-about Puruliya, every freedom fighter has a story. Very few of them get to tell it.

Scan QR code for PARI Freedom Fighters Gallery.

16

R. NALLAKANNU'S FIGHT FOR MANY FORGOTTEN FREEDOMS

'There were times during the freedom struggle, too, when things looked bleak. We were told you cannot win. You are up against the greatest empire in the world . . . But we rose above all those warnings and threats. And fought anyway. That's why we are here today.'

—R. Nallakannu, Chennai, Tamil Nadu

'Vote for the Yellow Box!' went the cries. 'Choose the auspicious *manjal petti*!'

This was Madras Presidency during the 1937 provincial elections held under British rule.

The slogans came from groups of youngsters beating drums. Most of them not of voting age. And ineligible to cast ballots even if they had been. Not all adults could vote.

Franchise restrictions favoured land and property owners and, in rural areas, rich farmers.

The sight of young people without a vote campaigning vigorously was not entirely new.

As early as July 1935, *Justice*—the newspaper and organ of the Justice Party—noted with disdain, and not a little contempt:

> You might visit any village even in outlying areas and you were sure to come across groups of urchins wearing Congress khaddar uniforms and Gandhi caps and holding aloft the tricoloured banner. Nearly eighty per cent of these men, workers and volunteers had been drawn from the voteless, propertyless, unemployed hundreds of the urban and village areas . . .

One of those youngsters in 1937 was R. Nallakannu, barely 12 at the time. Now 97 [in 2022], he's telling us of the drama, laughing about his having been one of those 'urchins'. 'Those who owned land and paid a land tax of ten rupees or more could vote,' he recalls. The 1937 polls did see some broadening of the franchise. But 'it was never meant to allow more than 15–20 per cent of adults to have a vote,' he says. 'And not more than 1,000 to 2,000 people voted in any one constituency.'

Nallakannu was 'born in Srivaikuntam, then in Tirunelveli district'. Today, the taluk of Srivaikuntam falls in Tamil Nadu's Thoothukudi district (which used to be called Tuticorin till 1997).

Nallakannu's activism, though, began early.

'When I was a child, in fact. Mill workers in Thoothukudi, close to my town, struck work. That was one of the Harvey Mills group. This came to be known as the Panchalai [Cotton Mills] workers' strike.

'To support them, rice would be collected from every home in our town and sent in boxes to the strikers' families in Thoothukudi. It was young boys like us who would go around to collect the rice.' People were poor, 'but every household contributed something. I was just 5 or 6 at the time, and this solidarity with the workers' struggle had a huge impact on me. It meant I would get used to involvement in politics quite early.'

We pull him back to the 1937 polls: What did he mean by voting for a *manjal petti* or yellow box?

'There were only two main parties in Madras then,' he says. 'Congress and the Justice Party. Instead of symbols, parties were identified by a ballot box of some colour. The Congress, for whom we then campaigned, was assigned a yellow box. For the Justice Party, there was a *pachchai petti*—green box. That was the best way at the time for the voter to identify which party he was supporting.'

And yes, there was much colour and theatre around the polls even then. *The Hindu* writes that 'Devadasi campaigner Thanjavur Kamukannamal . . . would ask everyone to vote in the "snuff box"'! Gold or yellow being a common colour for snuff boxes of the time. *The Hindu* itself carried a headline calling on readers to 'Fill the Yellow Boxes'.

'And of course, I could not vote at age 12,' says Nallakannu. 'But I went out and canvassed as strongly as I could.' Three years later, he would be involved in political campaigns beyond the electoral. And 'beating a *parai* (a type of drum) and yelling slogans'.

But he was no longer a Congress supporter. 'I was with the Communist Party of India [CPI] from age 15,' says Nallakannu, 'Comrade RNK' to his friends. Formal membership of the party would have to wait till he was older. But RNK would emerge one of the most important figures of the Communist movement in Tamil Nadu over the next few decades. He would be seeking—often successfully—support for the *sengodi* (red flag) and not the *manjal petti* (yellow box).

'There was only one school in our part of Tirunelveli and so it was simply called "School". That was its only name.'

Nallakannu is speaking to us in his small home office in Chennai. Beside him, on a sideboard of his table, are a bunch of little busts and small statuettes. Lenin, Marx and Periyar right next to him. Behind them, a bigger, golden statuette of Ambedkar that stands in front of a larger sketch of revolutionary Tamil poet Subramania Bharati. Behind the small Periyar bust is another sketch, drawn from a photo of Bhagat Singh, Rajguru and Sukhdev. And next to all these, a calendar that asks all of us to 'Use Less Water'.

The busts, statuettes and sketches on Nallakanu's sideboard tell
us his intellectual history at a glance.

The whole tableau captures, at a glance, the intellectual
development and history of the man we are in conversation
with for the third time. It is 25 June 2022. The first of our
interviews with him was in 2019.

'Bharathiyar was the most inspirational poet for me,' says
Nallakannu. 'Often his poems or songs were banned.' He cites
some lines from '*Suthinthara Pallu*' ('Independence Song'), an
extraordinary song by the poet. 'He wrote it, I think, in 1909.
So he celebrates independence thirty-eight years before India
attained it in 1947!'

We will dance, we will sing
For we have achieved the joy of independence

The time when we used to call Brahmins as 'Sir' has gone,
The time when we used to call the white men as 'lord' has gone,

The time when we saluted those who took alms from us has gone,
The time when we serve people who made fun of us has gone.
In all places the only talk is about freedom . . .

Bharathi died in 1921, four years before Nallakannu was born. The song was written even earlier. But it, and others, inspired him through his fighting years. RNK knew many songs and poems of Bharati before he was 12. He is able to recall quite a few of the verses and lyrics verbatim even today. 'I learnt some of those from the Hindi pundit Pallavesam Chettiar at school,' he says. And of course, none of those were on the official curriculum.

'I also got a book of Bharathiyar's writings from S. Satyamurti when he came to the school. It was a collection of his poems *Thesiya Geetham.*' Satyamurti was a freedom fighter, politician and a patron of the arts. Bharati was one of the first to acclaim the 1917 October Revolution in Russia and even wrote a song in its praise.

It's good to try and understand Nallakannu through his love for Bharati and the prism of the agrarian and working-class struggles he was part of for eight decades.

For it is really difficult to tell the story of 'Comrade RNK' otherwise. This is one of the most self-effacing souls I have ever met. He gently but firmly declines to place himself at the centre of any of the great events, strikes and struggles he tells us about. His role in some of those was vital and central all right. But you can never get him to portray or narrate it that way.

'Comrade RNK was one of the founding leaders of the farmers' movement in our state,' says G. Ramakrishnan. 'GR' is a state committee member of the CPI(M), but unreservedly salutes the role and contribution of the 97-year-old CPI leader. 'Through the decades—starting from when he was still a teenager—it was he who, along with Srinivas Rao, created the bases of the Kisan Sabha across the state. Those remain a source of the strength for the Left even today. And Nallakannu helped create that by tireless campaigns and struggles all across Tamil Nadu.'

Nallakannu's struggles seamlessly integrate farmers' battles with the anticolonial movement. And also, very importantly, with the anti-feudal battles that were so crucial to Tamil Nadu of that time. Those too flow over strongly post-1947. His fight was and remains one for many forgotten freedoms. Not just Independence from British rule.

'We'd fight them at night, throw stones—those were the weapons we had—and chase them away. Sometimes, there would be pitched battles. This happened several times during the protests that came in the 1940s. We were still boys, but we fought. Day and night, with our kind of weapons!'

Fight whom? And chase them away from what and where?

'The *uppalam* [salt pans] near my town. All the salt pans were under British control. The condition of the workers was miserable. Like around the mills, where the struggles began decades earlier. There were protests and there was a lot of public sympathy and support for them.

'The police simply functioned as the agents of the salt pan owners. In one clash, a sub-inspector died. There had even been an attack on the police station there. Then they set up a mobile patrolling unit. They would go to the pans during the day and come to camp near our villages at night. That's when we clashed with them.' These protests and clashes went on and off for a couple of years, maybe more. 'But it was around 1942 and the Quit India movement that they really grew.'

Nallakannu's taking part in all of this while barely a teenager did not go down well with his father Ramasamy Thevar. A farmer, Thevar owned some 4–5 acres of land and had six children. The young RNK was often punished at home. And sometimes his father would withhold paying his school fees.

'People would tell him—"Your son does not study? He's always out and shouting. Looks like he's gone and joined the Congress."' The deadline for paying the fees at 'School' fell between the 14th and 24th of each month. 'If I asked him for the fees, he'd shout at me: "You leave your studies and help your uncles on the farm."'

'As time ran out, someone close to my father would placate him. They would promise him that I would not speak and act the way I was doing. Only then would he pay the fees.'

However, 'the more he opposed my life, my ways, the deeper my dissent grew. I made it up to intermediate level in Tamil, at The Hindu College, Madurai. It was actually at the Tirunelveli junction. But it was called Hindu

College, Madurai. I only studied there two years. I couldn't go further.'

Because he was busy taking part in protests. And significantly—though he is far too modest to say it—he had even begun to organize them. RNK was swiftly emerging a young leader. But one who never sought, and mostly avoided, a high profile.

It's hard to keep a chronological track of the events and actions he was involved in. More so as they were many in number and occurred on quite different fronts.

He sums up the most important moments for him during the freedom struggle simply, though: 'The battles around the Quit India movement.' He was not yet 17 at that point, but already an important figure in the protests. The years between age 12 and 15 were also the time of his transition from Congressman to Communist.

What sort of protest meetings did he help organize or take part in?

Early on, 'we had megaphones made of tin. We'd gather any tables and chairs we could in a village or town and sing. Mainly the table was for the speaker to stand on and address the crowd. Mind you, crowds would unfailingly show up.' Once again, he says little about his own role in mobilizing people. Though it was foot soldiers like him who made that possible.

'Later, speakers like Jeevanandam would stand on those tables and talk to fairly large audiences. With no mikes. He did not need them.

'Over time, we began to get decent mikes and loudspeakers. The most favoured one,' he recalls, 'was what were called the "Chicago mikes". Or Chicago Radio systems. Of course, we could not afford them too often.'

What about when there was a British crackdown? How did they communicate then?

'There were many such situations. Like after the Royal Indian Navy [RIN] mutiny [1946]. There was a total crackdown on the Communists. But there were raids earlier too. And the British would sometimes search every party office in the villages. That happened even after Independence, by the way, when the party was banned. We did have bulletins and magazines. Like *Janashakti*, for instance. But we had other modes of communication. Some of those were simple signals going back centuries.

'Right from the time of Kattabomman [legendary eighteenth-century anti-British fighter], people used to place neem twigs at the entrance of a home. It was a sign to indicate that someone inside was sick with smallpox or other ailments. But it was also used as a secret symbol to signal that a meeting was going on there.

'If there were sounds of a baby crying inside the house, that meant the meeting was still on. If the cow dung near the entrance was wet, the meeting was still on. If the dung there was dry, it was a signal to turn away and leave, as danger lurked. Or meant that the meeting was over.'

What was RNK's greatest source of inspiration through the freedom struggle?

'The Communist Party was our greatest source of inspiration.'

'Why did I remove my moustache when I was arrested?' RNK laughs. 'I never did. And I never grew it to disguise my face in the first place. If that was the case, why should I have grown one at all?

'No, the police burnt it off with a cigarette. That was part of the torture inflicted on me by an Inspector Krishnamurthy from Madras city. He tied my hands at 2 a.m. He only untied them the next morning at 10. Then he beat me with his baton for a long time.'

Again, like many fellow freedom fighters, he recalls the incident with no personal rancour. No animosity towards his torturer. RNK never looked for the police inspector in later days to settle scores. It never once occurred to him to do so.

'This actually happened in 1948,' he says, after India attained Independence. 'The party had been banned in many provinces, including Madras, and remained that way till 1951.

'But you should understand there were also anti-feudal battles that had to be fought. That we had to pay a price for. And these began long before 1947—and continued well after Independence.

'Freedom movement, social reform, anti-feudal struggles—we combined these issues. That's how we worked.

We fought for better and equal wages. We fought for the abolition of untouchability. We played a serious role in the temple entry movements.

'The campaign for abolition of the zamindari system was a major movement in Tamil Nadu. The state had many important zamindaris. We fought the *mirasdari* [land held under hereditary title] and *inamdari* [lands assigned free to individuals or institutions by the ruler] systems. It was the Communists who were at the forefront of these battles. There were very major landlords to contend with, and their private armed goondas and thugs.

'There were people like Punniyoor Saambasiva Iyer, Nedumanam Saamiyappa Muthaliyaar, Poondi Vandiyar. They held thousands of acres of fertile land.'

We are now sitting in on a fascinating history lesson. From a man who helped make that history.

'There were also the centuries-old practices of *brahmatheyam* and *thevathaanam*.

'Under the first, lands were given for free to Brahmins by the rulers. They ruled and profited from the land. They would not directly cultivate it, but the profits would go to them. Under *thevathaanam,* such gifts of land would be made to temples. Sometimes a temple could be gifted an entire village. The small tenants and workers lived at their mercy. Anyone who stood up to them could and would be evicted.

'Know this, these institutions, the *madams* [mutts or monasteries] owned six lakh acres of land. Maybe even now. But their power has been strongly curtailed by people's unflinching struggles.

'The Tamil Nadu Zamindari Abolition Act came into force in 1948. But it was the zamindars and giant landowners who were compensated. Not the people who had worked the land for them. The affluent tenants got some compensation. The poor who worked in the fields got nothing. Between 1947–49, there were a large number of evictions from these temple lands. And we launched huge protests along the lines of: "Only when farmers own the land can they live well."

'These were our battles—and from 1948 to 1960, the fight went on for getting their rights. C. Rajagopalachari [Rajaji] as Chief Minister took the side of the landlords and mutts. We said, "Land to the Tiller". Rajaji said land belongs to those who have the documents. But our struggles saw us break that total power these temples and mutts had. We defied their harvest rules and protocols. We refused to be slaves.

'And, of course, all this could not be separated from the social battles as well.

'I remember witnessing one of the protests at a temple one night. The temples would all have chariot festivals. And it was the farmers who would pull the chariots forward with ropes. We said they will not come to pull the chariots anywhere if the evictions continued. We also asserted our right to take some of the grain back for sowing.'

Now he's moving back and forth between pre- and post-Independence periods. At one level, that's confusing. At another, it brings home the complexity of those times. That there were many freedoms involved. That some of these did not have clear start and end dates. That people like RNK remained steadfast in the pursuit of those freedoms.

'We also, right through those decades, fought against the beatings and torture of the workers.

'In 1943, Dalit workers were still being whipped. And having cow dung water poured on the wounds created by the whips. They had to go to work at 4 or 5 a.m. in the morning—whenever the rooster crowed. They had to be at the *mirasdars'* lands to bathe the cattle, gather the cow dung, then go to water the fields. There was a village near Thiruthuraipoondi then in Thanjavur district. That's where we held their protest.

'There was a huge demonstration headed by Srinivas Rao of the Kisan Sabha. The sentiment was "if they hit you for carrying the red flag, hit them back". Finally the *mirasdars* and Mudhaliars at Thiruthuraipoondi signed an agreement that this whipping, use of cow dung water and other barbaric practices would be stopped.'

RNK plays down his own huge role in these great battles all the way from the 1940s to the 1960s and well beyond. He would succeed Srinivas Rao as the head of the All-India Kisan Sabha (AIKS), Tamil Nadu. In the decades after 1947, the silent foot soldier would emerge a strong general in the battles of farmers and labourers.

Both of them are excited and emotional. We are doing one of our interviews at CPI(M) leader and freedom fighter N. Sankariah's house. That is, we're talking to both him and Nallakannu together. The way the comrades of eight decades greet each other touches the emotions of the rest of us in the room, too.

97-year-old Nallakannu greets his 101-year-old comrade, Sankariah, in Chennai.

Is there no bitterness, no sadness? They went their different ways when the Communist Party of India split into two over fifty years ago. It was not an amiable parting.

'But we have worked together on many issues and struggles even after that,' says Nallakannu. 'With the same attitude towards each other as from before.'

'When the two of us meet,' says Sankariah, 'we are still one party.'

How do they respond to the present-day rise in communal violence and hatred? Do they fear for the nation's survival? A nation whose independence they helped achieve.

'There were times during the freedom struggle, too, when things looked bleak,' says Nallakannu. 'We were told you cannot win. You are up against the greatest empire in the world. Some of our families were warned to keep us away from the struggle. But we rose above all those warnings and threats. And fought anyway. That's why we are here today.'

There is also the need, both of them say, to build broad unity. To reach out and learn from others as in the past. 'I think even an EMS [Namboodiripad] had a Gandhi photo in his room,' says RNK.

How do the two of them remain so calm and sanguine about the state of politics that so scares millions among the rest of us? Nallakannu shrugs: 'We've seen worse.'

Scan QR code for PARI Freedom Fighters Gallery.

A MEMORY

'Do you remember me?' the elderly Scotsman asked my grandfather.

Thathayya (Telugu for grandfather) stared at him, certain he was someone he had known in another era, but couldn't place him.

'I know you, I'm sure,' he said, 'but I'm struggling to remember your name.'

The old gentleman rose and gave Thathayya a narrow strip of cloth with some numbers on it. Thathayya took one look at it—and burst out laughing.

He now remembered the man. 'Why did you keep this?' he asked, still laughing, and looking at the strip of cloth he held in his hands.

'I had my eye on you and a few others I thought would make something of their lives,' said the elderly Scot. 'I retained those numbers for about six or seven of you.'

Turning to us kids, he said, 'I had your grandfather in prison—be good.'

He had been my grandfather's jail warden some three decades earlier. And had now come around to give him his convict number, which he had retained as a souvenir.

His visit had made Thathayya's day—but left me a little stunned.

It's disconcerting—when you're not fully 4 years old—to learn that your grandfather had been a jailbird. A convict who had spent several years in prison.

And besides, how come he, a former prisoner, was such an important person now?

I demanded an explanation.

Thathayya kept looking at the strip of cloth and the numbers after his former jail warden had left. His eyes were moist and his mind preoccupied. But he tried responding to me. Not so much immediately, as over a period of years and several conversations—for I had many questions.

And so began my journey of learning about India's freedom struggle. My grandfather had spent many years in British jails. Before which he had been deported from Ireland, where he was studying law. He was active in Indian groups that campaigned against British rule. And he had gotten too close to Irish revolutionaries who would play a crucial role in the 1916 Easter Uprising in that country. On 1 June 1916, he was given a month's notice to leave Ireland and the United Kingdom.

On returning to India, he threw himself into the national movement here. He was one of those who gained from his participation in it. There was almost no period after Independence, till 1974 when he went into retirement, that he did not hold some public office of power. He died in 1980.

I grew more and more curious about the millions he often mentioned, saying it was ordinary people who really made Independence possible. Not elites like himself.

Who were those people, I wondered. As I grew up, I realized that some of them would drop in now and then to meet him. I never tired of hearing their stories, learning about their lives.

They and millions like them had fought and sacrificed for India's freedom. With little or no reward. I met more of them as I went through college. At university, I studied history— and found that almost all the great uprisings against the British began in the rural areas, not the cities.

Among the things I learnt: In 1857, elites in the cities of Calcutta and Bombay (now Kolkata and Mumbai) actively supported the British. They even organized meetings to pray for the colonizer's success. That unfolded even as thousands of Indian soldiers in the colonial army turned against the British. Then as now, the Indian soldier was in essence a kisan in uniform. They could not but reflect the mood of their villages gripped by agrarian despair.

I also learnt, over decades, of the uprising led by Veer Narayan Singh in Chhattisgarh—starting a year before 1857. Of the incredible Ghadar revolt of 1913–15 centred in Punjab. Of the third Rampa Rebellion of 1922–24, led by

Alluri Sitarama Raju, in Andhra Pradesh. Of many more such episodes in our history.

In 1997, as India turned fifty, I visited villages where some of the most heroic struggles against the mightiest empire in the world had begun. Sonakhan in Chhattisgarh. Rampachodavaram in Andhra Pradesh. Kalliasseri in Kerala and others. I wrote a series on them called 'Forgotten Freedoms' in *The Times of India* to mark the fiftieth year of Indian Independence.

This book is an effort to bring to readers the stories of some of our forgotten freedom fighters. This time, in the seventy-fifth year of India's Independence.

Stories we need to know.

Sure, fifteen to sixteen individuals—a few of them still alive—that's a very small number. But they were and are representative of the many unknown millions who fought for India's freedom and independence.

I had from 1993, the year I went into rural reporting full-time, run into ageing fighters in villages across the country. In them, every single time, I found the extraordinary in the ordinary. Over the next many years, I tried to meet and interview them, and record their stories. But failed to do that consistently. The agrarian crisis took centre stage from the late 1990s. And my focus as rural affairs editor of *The Hindu*, a post I held from 2004–14, was driven by farm distress. Still, I managed to meet with and even revisit some of these fighters or their descendants—and their villages.

A Memory

The first round of village visits entirely for these stories began in 2002. In subsequent years, there were many occasions where I ran into or found freedom fighters in rural India while working on something else. The last round of visits I made to some of these villages was in March and April 2022.

And that's how this book came about.

ANNEXURE I

For Demati Sabar 'Salihan'
They won't tell your story, Salihan
And I can't see you making Page 3
That's for the painted whatnot,
the liposuctioned lot,
the rest's for the Captains of Industry

Prime Time's not for you, Salihan
It is, and this isn't funny,
for those who murder and maim
who burn and who blame
And speak saintly then, of Harmony

The Brits torched your village, Salihan
So many men carrying guns
They came by the train

bringing terror and pain
Till sanity itself was undone

They burnt all there was, Salihan
after looting the cash and the grain
Brutes of the Raj
led a violent charge
But you faced them with total disdain

You strode down the street towards him
you faced that man with the gun
In Saliha they still tell the story
of the battle you fought
and you won

Your kin lay bleeding around you
your father, a bullet in his leg
Still, you stood tall,
Drove those Brits to the wall
For you went there to fight, not to beg

You struck that officer, Salihan
And thrashed him before he could move
When he finally did
he limped and he hid
seeking refuge from 16-year-old you

Forty girls against the Raj, Salihan
And strong and beautiful, too
Now you're shrunk and you're grey,
your body withers away
But there's a spark in those eyes that's still you

Those who toadied the Raj, Salihan,
they rule your poor village today
And build temples of stone
but they'll never atone
for bartering our freedoms away

You die as you lived, Salihan
Hungry, with little to eat
In history's shades
your memory, it fades,
like Raipur Jail's roster sheets

Had I but your heart, Salihan
What success would I then not see?
Though that battle itself
was not for yourself
But that your people might also be free

Our children should know you, Salihan
But what is your claim to fame?
No ramp did you glide

No crown wear with pride
Nor lend Pepsi and Coke your name

Do speak to me, Salihan
For endless an hour as you please
This hack, when we part,
wants to write of your heart
Not romance India's Captains of Sleaze

These are the verses I mentioned in the chapter 'When Demati Dei "Salihan" Took on the Raj'. On a story done in such detail over years, I did not want to impose my angry scribbles in verse of that time—twenty years ago. The story was to be about her, and not shift focus to the author. So, it was not part of the story. Here, I include it as an annexure because it was part of that experience and reflects the anger and outrage of all of us who met her, and found her in the condition we did, that day in 2002.

REFERENCES

Artha. 'Market Prices in Mumbai: Weekly Retail Market Prices', 19 August 1943. Year 9, Issue 34, 25 August 1943, https://dspace.gipe.ac.in/xmlui/bitstream/handle/10973/31683/artha-09-34.pdf?sequence=2&isAllowed=y.

Atalury, Murali. 'Alluri Sitarama Raju, and the Manyam Rebellion of 1922–1924'. *Social Scientist*, Vol. 12, No. 4, April 1984, pp. 3–33.

Baker, Christopher. 'The Congress at the 1937 Elections in Madras'. *Modern Asian Studies*, Vol. 10, No. 4 (London: Cambridge University Press), 1976. https://www.jstor.org/stable/311763?seq=18#metadata_info_tab_contents.

Bharati, Subramaniam. '*Aaduvome pallu paduvome*' C. Song, 1909. http://www.hindupedia.com/en/Aaduvome_pallu_paduvome.

Chandra, Bipan, Mridula Mukherjee, Aditya Mukherjee, Sucheta Mahajan, and K. N. Pannikar. *India's Struggle for*

Independence. New Delhi: Penguin Random House India, 2016.

Chopra, P. N. *Who's Who of Indian Martyrs*, Vol. 1, *1857–1947*. New Delhi: Division MoIB, Government of India, 2016.

Datta, K. K. *History of the Freedom Movement in Bihar*, Vol. 3, *1942–47*. Patna: Government of Bihar, 1958. https://www.indianculture.gov.in/flipbook/8655.

Gandhi, M. K. *Collected Works of Mahatma Gandhi*, XLV (December 1930–April 1931). Item 131, 'Letter to Prema Kantak from Yerawada Central Jail, January 17, 1931'. New Delhi: Ministry of Information and Broadcasting, 1971, pp. 95. https://www.gandhiheritage portal.org/cwmg_volume_thumbview/NDU=#page/130/mode/2up.

Gandhi, M. K. *Collected Works of Mahatma Gandhi*, XII (April 1913–December 1914). Item 385, 'London Speech August 8, 2014'. New Delhi: Ministry of Information and Broadcasting, 1971, pp. 523–26. https://www.gandhiheritage portal.org/cwmg_volume_thumbview/MTI=#page/564/mode/2up.

Ghosh, Niranjan. *Role of Women in the Freedom Movement in Bengal, 1919–1947: Midnapore, Bankura, and Purulia District*. India: Tamralipta Prakashani, 1988.

Giri, V. V. *My Life and Times*. Delhi: The Macmillan Company of India Limited, 1976.

Verma, Rajendra, ed. *Madhya Pradesh District Gazetteer for Raipur 1973*. Government of Madhya Pradesh, 1973.

Guha, Abhijit. 'An Early Freedom Struggle That Is Still Not Free of the "Chuar" Label'. *Forward Press*, 10 July 2018. https://www.forwardpress.in/2018/07/an-early-freedom-struggle-that-is-still-not-free-of-the-chuar-label/.

Habib, Irfan. *The National Movement*, Part 2, *The Struggle for Freedom*. New York: Columbia University Press, 2020.

The Hindu. 'Communist Leader N. Sankaraiah to Receive Thagaisal Thamizhar Award', 28 July 2022. https://www.thehindu.com/news/national/tamil-nadu/communist-leader-n-sankaraiah-to-receive-thagaisal-thamizhar-award/article35577463.ece.

Hobsbawm, Eric. *Bandits*. London: Abacus, 2001.

Lal, Chaman, ed. *The Bhagat Singh Reader*. Noida: HarperCollins, 2019.

Lalita, K., Vasantha Kannabiran, Rama Melkote, Uma Maheshwari, Susie Tharu, and Veena Shatrugna. *We Were Making History: Life Stories of Women in the Telangana People's Struggle*. *Book by Stree Shakti Sanghatana*. New Delhi: Kali for Women, 1989.

Menon, Parvathi. *Breaking Barriers: Stories of Twelve Women*. New Delhi: LeftWord Books, 2004.

Mohan, S. and D. Ramakrishnan. 'Political History of Thiru R. Nallakannu in Tamil Nadu—A Study', *Education and Society*, Vol. 5, No.1, January–December 2016 (New Delhi: APH Publishing Corporation), pp. 139–44.

Ota, A. B. and S. C. Mohanty, H. B. Barad. *BHUMIJ*. Bhubaneswar: Scheduled Castes and Scheduled Tribes Research and Training Institute (SCSTRTI), 2014.

https://tribal.nic.in/repository/ViewDoc.aspx?Repository No=TRI28-08-2017121302&file=Docs/TRI28-08-2017121302.pdf.

Panda, Saraja Kumar. 'Freedom Fighters of Panimara', *Orissa Review,* Government of Odisha, January 2006. http:// magazines.odisha.gov.in/Orissareview/jan2006/engpdf/ Freedom_Fighters_of_Panimara.pdf.

Patankar, Vilas. *Krantisinh Nana Patil: A Forever Revolutionary* (in Marathi). Mumbai: Maharashtra Literary and Cultural Society, 2002.

Paneeru, Ramesh. *Telangana Armed Struggle—In Nalgonda District. A Case Study of Kadavendi Village 1930–52 A.D.* Hyderabad: Prajashakti Book House, 2010.

Parthasarathy, Rangaswami. *Journalism in India: From the Earliest Times to the Present Day.* New Delhi: Sterling Publishers, 1997.

Powar, Vilas. *Makers of Maharashtra: Leading Revolutionary G. D. Bapu Lad—Life and Work* (in Marathi). Mumbai: Maharashtra Literary and Cultural Society, 2017.

Punyavati, S. 'Swarajyam, a Fallen Flower in the Orchard of Red Blossoms'. *People's Democracy,* 3 April 2022. https:// peoplesdemocracy.in/2022/0403_pd/swarajyam-fallen-flower-orchard-red-blossoms.

Puri, Harish K. *Ghadar Movement: A Short History.* New Delhi: National Book Trust, 2011.

Ramkrishnan, N. P. *Ramamurti: A Centenary Tribute.* Chennai: Bharathi Puthakalayam, 2008.

Sharma, B. K. *Peasant Movement in Rajasthan, 1920–1949.* Jaipur: Pointer Publishers, 1999.

Sharma, B. K. *Mass Movements and Freedom Struggle in Rajasthan (1818–1949).* Jodhpur: Rajasthani Granthagar, 2013.

Singh, Bhagat. *Jail Notebooks and Other Writings.* New Delhi: LeftWord Books, 2007.

Waraich, Malwinder Jit Singh and Harinder Singh. *Ghadr Movement Original Documents*: Volume 1. A. Mohali-Chandigarh: Unistar Books, 2014.

Sriram, V. 'When Madras First Voted'. *The Hindu,* 25 April 2014. https://www.thehindu.com/features/metroplus/society/when-madras-first-voted/article5946786.ece.

Sundarayya, P. *Telangana People's Struggle and Its Lessons.* New Delhi: Cambridge University Press, 2006.

Swatantrata Sainik Samman Pension Scheme, 1980: Citizen Charter. Ministry of Home Affairs. https://www.mha.gov.in/sites/default/files/Swatantrata_sainik_27102016.PDF.

Venkataraman, V. *Swadeshism and Nationalism in Colonial Tamilnadu, 1905–1947.* Chennai: New India Publishing House, 2021.

ACKNOWLEDGEMENTS

First and foremost—my gratitude and thanks to the freedom fighters in this book and their families for their trust, tolerance and generosity. For the amount of time they gave me, the number of visits and interviews (and follow-ups) they put up with. Above all, for the frank, honest and unreserved sharing of their lives. That's a debt I can never repay.

Their families continue to help me, ferreting out old documents, letters, photographs and more. Almost all the fighters were or are from very poor families—and most have no photographs of themselves or their kin prior to 1947. Yet, they went out and tried getting me some pics of that period from friends, relatives and others.

The earliest—limited version—of one of these stories on the Badmash Gaon appeared in *The Hindu Sunday Magazine* in 2002. My thanks to Nirmala Lakshman, then its editor, for enthusiastically supporting the pursuit of that story, which was published in two parts. The response we got—surely due to her front-page projection of the piece—made me believe this could be a big series.

The earliest, much shorter, versions of the stories on Laxmi Panda and Baji Mohammad appeared on the op-ed page of *The Hindu*. The idea of a series itself was badly disrupted by the fact that, as the Rural Affairs Editor of that daily, I was completely caught up in covering the agrarian crisis, eventually doing 200 or more reports on its different aspects. But I still managed to meet many of the freedom fighters while visiting the villages and covering rural distress and the farm suicides.

The old fighters I met during some of those visits shared deep insights, not just about the freedom struggle but about rural distress itself. I was taught how the agrarian crisis was inevitable in the way our nation had moved away from its freedom struggle ideals.

None of the above, whether covering the agrarian crisis itself or the fighters, would have been possible but for the unwavering support of N. Ram, then Editor-in-Chief of *The Hindu*. He gave me total freedom to travel and write as I wished. He allowed me to build a rural India platform that saw reports of the crisis always highlighted and sometimes front-paged. The experience, insights, knowledge and confidence that brought me—my thanks to Ram for that. And for backing all I did so unstintingly. His contribution to my growth as a journalist across thirty years goes way beyond this book.

Research and travel for this book were supported by a Senior Fellowship from Tricontinental: Institute for Social

Research. A few of the stories (like those on Captain Bhau, Hausabai Patil, Ganpati Bal Yadav and Bhabani Mahato) appeared in much shorter form in the People's Archive of Rural India (PARI). It was the wild enthusiasm and response of my colleagues at PARI that pushed me to do many more (some of which are published for the first time ever in this book).

The list of editors and 'auditors' I have to thank is, well, huge.

Let me begin by thanking my patient and tolerant editor at Penguin, Karthik Venkatesh. I'm betting he was relieved when the process of dealing with a reporter who simply couldn't resist adding a new story now and then, even as the book was being prepared, came to an end. Karthik coped in grace with a disorganized, anarchistic author. As did Meru Gokhale, Penguin's Publisher, with my repeated violation of deadlines—and whose decision it was in the first place to not just go in for this book but to move on it quickly so that it could come out in the seventy-fifth year of India's Independence.

My sincere thanks to Penguin designer Ahlawat Gunjan and illustrator Amit Srivastava for the beautiful cover this book has. The people in the illustration—drawn from an old, hazy picture (c. 1943)—are Toofan Sena troops. Note that the ordinary troopers are literally 'foot soldiers'—most have no shoes.

A very special thanks to my old teacher Professor Romila Thapar. The questions she raised on the first draft of the first story in this book had me scrambling to find answers that would eventually affect at least two other stories in it. Simply put: Those questions made a vital difference to me. As did her generous comments on it, on reading the manuscript.

The editors of the earliest versions included Shalini Arun in *The Hindu Sunday Magazine* and P. V. Sitapathi in *The Hindu*. In the stories appearing in PARI, Sharmila Joshi's deft and skilful edits made, as always, a worthwhile difference.

Since I think—if you believe in storytelling in the way I do—that a piece needs to be checked for how it *sounds*, and how it comes across when reading aloud for different age groups, the following 'auditors' were forced to suffer more than one guinea pig audio session: Anushree Ramanathan, Aparna Karthikeyan, Archana Shukla, Kavitha Iyer, Kavitha Muralidharan, Namita Waikar, Oorna Raut, Pratishtha Pandya, Priti David, Purusottam Thakur, Ritayan Mukherjee, Sangeeta Menon, Smita Khator, Vinutha Mallya and Vishaka George. (And earlier, when some of the stories were in much shorter form in PARI, colleagues like Parth M. N.) All of them are colleagues at or contributors to PARI, and their inputs were simply invaluable. I made significant changes in the structure of a few of the stories based on the comments of Aparna, Archana, Pratishtha, Smita and Sangeeta. Especially so in a few stories pored over by Sangeeta, who was also extremely helpful in the final edits and checks and picked out errors and confusing stuff far sooner than I would have myself. Thanks to Pratistha Pandya, who also helped correct and reorganize the references. And thanks to Kanika Gupta, who took on most of my workload in PARI's latest project on the art of Adivasi children. That helped me focus on the book. My gratitude also, to PARI photo editor Binaifer Bharucha, who has worked so hard on so many of the photographs I shot of freedom fighters.

Outside the PARI network, my dear friends Professor Robert Jensen in New Mexico, USA, and Professor Robin Jeffrey in Melbourne, Australia, read and criticized the manuscript (one story at a time!) most usefully. Robin raised questions that made a major difference to the Captain Bhau story. And it felt great to have dear old friends Adam and Arlie Hochschild in Berkeley, CA, read and critique some of the stories. All their comments were invaluable.

So were those of Professor Jayati Ghosh in India—whom I bombarded with some of these stories. And who always gives me great advice on economics and numbers problems—and did so this time, too. Also, my old friend and former student Priyanka Kakodkar, who was the original 'auditor' for *Everybody Loves a Good Drought*. Thanks too, to Amrita Chakraborty, Anindita Mukherjee, Sheetal Chhabria and Sudhanva Deshpande. A big thanks to Gopal Gandhi for guiding me to what M. K. Gandhi had to say on the role of ordinary people in making history and revolution. And even more for his generous appreciation of this work on reading the manuscript.

A very special thanks to Sanchith Shivakumar and Sriya Sridhar, both young lawyers in Chennai, Tamil Nadu. Sanchith undertook the awful job of decoding the legalese drowning the pension schemes for freedom fighters. His analysis of it actually helped shape my own understanding of that subject. A suggestion from Sriya saw me restructure the introduction to this book—for the better.

And many thanks to my friends at Swecha—Praveen Chandrahas, Bhuvan Krishna and Akhila Matathammal—for setting up the QR codes linking the stories to the PARI site, and for helping create the Freedom Fighters Gallery there.

Satara and Sangli, Maharashtra

My sincere thanks to the late Captain Bhau of the Toofan Sena, his wife Kalpana Lad and their family. What an extraordinary couple! He allowed us to take his personal chair from his home and seat him on it at the site of the Shenoli train attack. Also to his indefatigable grandson, Advocate Deepak Lad, who enabled us to have continued contact with the old warrior. Every year from 2016, on Captain Bhau's birthday, Deepak would call and put me on the phone with him. My thanks to Balasaheb Ganpati Shinde, a follower of the Captain, for helping us at the Shenoli site.

Like with Bhau and Kalpana, I am sad to record my thanks to Hausabai Patil—after her passing. Her sharp sense of humour, her brilliant mind—what a pleasure it was to interact with her! And what a firebrand she must have been when confronting the Raj between 1943 and 1946! Many, many thanks to her family—particularly to her son, Advocate Subhash Patil, who patiently took a huge number of calls and conveyed all my follow-up questions to Hausabai after she slowed down with age and illness. Her story, which is the first one in this book, owes much to Subhash Patil.

Acknowledgements

Ganpati Bal Yadav too has died, and how I wish all those above could have been around to receive a copy of this book— which they had looked forward to. I will never forget him. A man who at 97 cycled 30 kilometres on the day we met him in 2018. His mild, self-effacing personality concealed the soul of a rebel who had been a courier and an enforcer for the *prati sarkar* and Toofan Sena. My thanks also to his family, especially his sons Nivrutti and Mahadeo.

A million thanks to journalist Sampat More, our friend in Shirgaon, who led me to Ganpati Yadav.

A very special thanks to Arun Lad, Chairman of the Kranti Sugar Cooperative and son of the legendary freedom fighter G. D. Bapu Lad. All three Toofan Sainiks in this book, Captain Bhau, Hausabai Patil and Ganpati Yadav, looked up to Bapu Lad as their mentor and leader. He, a founder of the Toofan Sena, led one squad in the attack on the train at Shenoli, while Captain Bhau led the other. Bapu Lad was the mastermind of the operation.

Arun Lad helped us with everything that we did with the freedom fighters, including organizing the 2017 felicitation of the still-living fighters of Satara and Sangli. He is a former member of the Maharashtra Legislative Assembly, a close friend of all three Toofan Sainiks in this book and a distant relative of Captain Bhau and Hausabai.

One of the greatest regrets I have in this entire endeavour is that I did not manage a personal, detailed interview with Bapu Lad. I had met him (and full disclosure: received a prize in his name) and was all set to make him one of the main figures in this book. But he died not very long after our meeting.

My thanks to Ashok Dhawale of the All-India Kisan Sabha (AIKS), who was the first person to put me in touch with the families of freedom fighters in Maharashtra, starting with those of the late Dada Undalkar and Bapu Lad. The AIKS Sangli and Umesh Deshmukh, state treasurer of the AIKS, were also co-organizers of the 2017 meeting to felicitate the freedom fighters of Satara and Sangli.

None of the Toofan Sena stories in this book would have happened had it not been for my dear friend and colleague Bharat Patil. Bharat set up our first meeting with Captain Bhau after we heard rumours of his being still alive. He also interpreted at the first interview with Bhau—often adding valuable points—at the very place on the railway track where the Captain and G. D. Bapu Lad had led the attack on the train carrying a payroll of the British Raj in 1943. It was after meeting Bhau in 2016 that we began to find the other Toofan Sainiks.

Sinchita Maji, Shreya Katyayini and Samyukta Shastri (all from PARI) shot extraordinary video footage and photographs of Captain Bhau and his family. They did that again at the public felicitation of freedom fighters of Satara and Sangli in 2017. Also on that trip with us to the felicitation were PARI's Siddharth Adelkar and Zahra Latif, always a help. My thanks to Archana Phadke for editing the video story on Captain Bhau that went up on PARI.

At the first interview with Hausabai Patil in Vita, Shreya Katyayini shot the main video footage, and Sinchita and

Samyukta took photographs. I simply could not have done that story but for the Marathi interviewing skills of PARI's Namita Waikar and the transcription and translation skills of Samyukta. Namita's help in the whole process has been greater than I can measure.

At the main interview with Ganpati Bal Yadav, Sinchita Maji and Sanket Jain shot extraordinary video footage of the 97-year-old cyclist for the shorter version of his story that was published on PARI. Both also shot great photos for the story, while Samyukta and Namita helped conduct the interview in Marathi. Both, again, were of immeasurable help in transcription and translation. Not just with the three in this book, but with the interviews of other Toofan Sainiks as well.

My thanks to PARI's Medha Kale, who discovered that wonderful resource *Artha*, a newsletter on economics in Marathi (going back to the 1930s) that gave me the most authentic figures on rice prices in Maharashtra in the times of the Toofan Sena. Medha also accompanied me on my trip to Kundal for the last meeting I was to ever have with Captain Bhau, who died in February 2022. Her help with confirming facts and numbers on the Toofan Sena's attacks was invaluable. As was that of Chandrakant Rokade and Arun Lad. My thanks to Comrade Laxman Bapu Dhankar of the All-India Kisan Sabha who, at age 95, shared his recollections of the price rise of that period with me.

I'm also grateful to Pankaj Bolar, our superb driver, who has taken us thousands of kilometres across Maharashtra to cover the freedom fighters and many other subjects.

Saliha, Purena, Panimora, Jeypore and Nabarangpur in Odisha

How does one ever thank the fearless freedom fighter Salihan—now that she's gone—for just tolerating our bursting in on her home? My interviews with Salihan took place in September 2002 on visits to her residence in Purena and with people in Saliha (the village she came from). On that trip I was accompanied by Purusottam Thakur, Jagadish Suna and Bijay Sahis. She was in bad shape, half-starving, losing her memory, and yet she treated us with great kindness and to a smile she lost just once when telling us the story of how the British police shot her father, Kartik Sabar.

In March 2022, I revisited Purena in Bargarh district and Saliha in Nuapada district along with Purusottam. We did detailed interviews with her relatives in both villages. Particularly, with Kulamani Bhoi, Hemanta Bhoi, Jasabanta Bhoi and Phagulal Bhoi in Purena. And with Menghraj Sabar, Ganpat Sabar and Bhanatram Sabar in Saliha. I also interviewed Mahesh Ram Sahu, President of the Salihagarh Shaheed Smriti Parishad.

I am most grateful to Jitamitra Prasad Singh Deo, historian and former ruler of the erstwhile Khariar zamindari in Nuapada. His knowledge of the anti-British revolts in that period is vast.

My gratitude, too, to Fanindam Singh Deo, author, historian and former principal of the Khariar Autonomous College in Nuapada, for giving me many insights into and a sharp analysis of the social, political and economic history of Nuapada and the Kalahandi region in the century before Independence.

My thanks also to Bibhudatta Guru, journalist from Nuapada, for his help in tracing Salihan's descendants in Salihagarh village.

I shall never forget that gentle soul Baji Mohammad, a Gandhian dedicated to non-violence to the last, who died in 2019 aged 103. Kindness and concern radiated from his being. After the interview in 2007, we could not stop talking about his complete lack of bitterness or anger towards the British, who incarcerated him in appalling conditions. Or towards the Sangh Parivar elements who fractured his skull while he sat in peaceful protest outside the Babri Masjid in 1992.

My thanks, too, to his nephew, Advocate Sirazuddin Ahmed and his family, in Nabarangpur town of Odisha's Nabarangpur district. It was Siraz who took us to the miserable cell where Baji had been imprisoned. And to the statue, a bust of Baji's, consigned to a bypass road where few will ever see it.

Laxmi Panda, too, is no more. I will never forget that simple, humble yet determined character. My thanks to those members of her family who met and helped us in March 2022, including her son Surendra Panda, his wife Sujata and three of their children—Bobby, Munna and Tobbu.

I was led to Laxmi Panda's story in 2007 by the extraordinary journalist Paresh Rath in Jeypore, Koraput. Nobody I know was a greater help to Laxmi—and to me in my pursuit of her story.

Acknowledgements

He was the journalist to first break her story—on ETV Odia National. Followed by Purusottam Thakur on NDTV Hindi.

In Panimora, the Badmash Gaon, I guess we'd have to thank dozens of people. But mainly the four freedom fighters Chamaru Parida, Jitendra Pradhan, Dayanidhi Nayak and Madan Bhoi. They were great storytellers. Particularly Chamaru who, at 91 in 2002, narrated the story of their capture of the Sambalpur court in 1942 with great humour and fun.

My thanks to the sons of Chamaru Parida, Gagan Bihari and Subira Parida, who gave us insights into their family's history. And to Kishore Chandra Pradhan, nephew of Jitendra Pradhan, the last of Panimora's freedom fighters to die—in January 2022, aged 102.

My thanks to PARI's Siddhita Sonavane, who transcribed the audio recordings of conversations with Jitamitra Prasad Singh Deo in Nuapada and Paresh Rath in Jeypore. There are four stories in this book from Odisha, the largest for any state that I've been to. These were also places I went back to across many years. In every instance, it all worked out because of my friend and colleague Purusottam Thakur, one of the finest journalists I have known in thirty years.

With him accompanying me on all our trips, we also spoke to large numbers of ordinary villagers other than the main protagonists in these stories. Including neighbours of the freedom fighters' families. And not just in Odisha—I was able to do that kind of search in Vidarbha thanks to Jaideep Hardikar. He did seek out living freedom fighters for me in that region, but the stories didn't work.

All the logistics, the arrangements, the contacting, the search for and tracing of the freedom fighters in Odisha happened because Purusottam was with me. Besides which, he was the Odia interpreter for every one of the interviews I ever did in these villages. I can never thank him enough.

Hyderabad, Telangana

I feel very bad when I remember freedom fighter Mallu Swarajyam asking when this book would come out. She last asked me that in October 2021. She died in March 2022. She will always rank in the top five most unforgettable characters I have ever met. This was one fearless, fiery and honest soul. Every time I spoke to her, I felt awed and inspired at the same time.

I interviewed Mallu Swarajyam three times. In September 2014, July 2018 and October 2021. The first of those interviews was recorded on video by Red Bangle Entertainment for ThoughtWorks Inc. I interviewed Swarajyam on stage for 1,500 techies assembled in a Hyderabad auditorium.

We also had an important conversation with her in the speakers' lounge of that event. The second interview, a much briefer one, took place on 17 July 2018.

The last and the most detailed one was conducted on 29 October 2021 and was almost fully recorded on video by Hyderabad videographer Stalin. I'd also made notes at a couple of her speeches in Telangana. I could not have, with my poor Telugu, handled the third interview without the assistance of my friend C. Sunita Reddy. My gratitude to Sunita, who also did that very difficult job—and transcription and translation of the video interview—wonderfully well.

I would also like to thank researcher and activist Dr K. Lalitha, who simultaneously and brilliantly translated the onstage interview of 2014 for the many non-Telugu speakers in the auditorium. Her translation captured both the spirit and context of what Swarajyam was saying.

And thanks, too, to PARI's Siddhita Sonavane, who transcribed the English subtitles which were part of a video within the video recording of the event in Hyderabad.

My thanks to Professor K. Nagaraj, who helped me understand and express the value of the bounty on Swarajyam's head in 1946 in present-day terms. Nagaraj had helped me understand the social context of numbers even when I was writing *Everybody Loves a Good Drought*. Thanks, too, to Thejaswi Puthraya, who has helped out every time I have looked for those number-commodity analogies.

I learnt a lot from speaking to Swarajyam's comrades in the CPI(M). Particular thanks to Konduri Veeraiah in Hyderabad, who dug up answers to my many queries and found several further references to her life in the 1940s. Also to Vinay Kumar of Prajashakti, who helped set up the last interview. In earlier years, I had also visited several of the villages Swarajyam was active in during the 1940s. And thanks to my dear friend Narasimha Reddy of *Eenadu*, who helped me get some old, historic photos of Swarajyam.

Chepua, Pirra and Matyala (in Puruliya, West Bengal)

My undying gratitude to freedom fighters Bhabani Mahato in Chepua and Thelu Mahato and Lokkhi Mahato in Pirra village of Puruliya, West Bengal. They were incredibly generous with their time and in sharing their life stories. And all of them were so inspiring, not just in the way they spoke—but in their vigour, youthfulness and spirit too. Two of them, Bhabani and Thelu, are already centenarians. Lokkhi is 97. I will count 26 March 2022, the day I wrapped up all their interviews, as one of the best days I've had in years.

My thanks, too, to Banalata Mahato, 96 years old, in Matyala village of Manbazar 1 block, Puruliya. Another completely understated freedom fighter—and a person who has never been recognized as being one.

They too are waiting for this book—and I intend to reach them with copies of it the week it is out.

My special thanks to Partha Sarathi Mahato, schoolteacher and Bhabani's grandson, who took us to her and to Banalata. And who pitched in with major revelations during the interviews we did with both. Besides, Partha *da* helped out in the meetings with Thelu and Lokkhi. Also chipping in usefully in that meeting was Sishir Kumar Mahato, a grand-nephew of freedom fighter Magaram Mahato. And Dinabandhu Mahato, grandson of Magaram.

Sincere thanks to Thelu's wonderful neighbours Amol, Shubhankar and Maumita Mahato. I'm grateful to them for their hospitality—and for their loving treatment of Thelu.

All that we did in Puruliya would not have been possible but for my PARI colleagues Smita Khator and Joshua Bodhinetra. More than a month before I went there, they had made a trip from Kolkata to Pirra and done a detailed pre-interview with Thelu and Lokkhi. The rich material they brought from that trip made my own interviews a snip. Smita, who accompanied me on my trip there, was not just knowledgeable, but also a brilliant interpreter who was able to put all the four main people we interviewed at total ease. I don't believe I could have persuaded Lokkhi to sing. She did. Smita also helped with follow-up queries rapidly and most effectively. Thanks, Smita and Joshua.

Ramgarh, Hoshiarpur and Jalandhar, Punjab

I can never thank enough the family of freedom fighter Bhagat Singh Jhuggian in Ramgarh, Hoshiarpur district, Punjab. I had, of course, thanked him profusely after the interview in August 2021. I was able to do that a second time at the *'Mela Gadri Babeyan Da'* in the grounds of the Desh Bhagat Yaadgar Hall, Jalandhar, in November 2021. I was so proud to share a stage with him on that occasion. But I cannot place this book in his hands. He died in March 2022.

My particular thanks to his wife Gurdev Kaur, a fearless activist in her own right, and son Paramjit Singh. They too, shared the story of Bhagat Singh Jhuggian—and their own experiences of and with him, generously.

Acknowledgements

And speaking of generosity, how am I ever going to thank Professor Jagmohan Singh of Ludhiana and Kuldip Singh, professor of education at Punjabi University, Patiala?

Professor Jagmohan has written the most informative (and kind) foreword to this book. It was also he who educated me a lot about the revolutionaries of the Punjab. And who better than the nephew of the legendary Bhagat Singh to do that? Professor Jagmohan also drove me to Jhuggian's house in Ramgarh. His presence put Jhuggian at ease. It is no exaggeration to say that every door in Punjab opens to you—if you are with Jagmohan Singh. He also reintroduced me to the extraordinary work of Professor Harish Puri on the Ghadar Party and movement.

Professor Kuldip Singh has organized almost every trip I've made to Punjab in the past four years. His astonishing network and range of contacts led me to people and places I had never known and who knew nothing of me. There is no measuring the contribution that Kuldip Singh, he of the boundless energy and enthusiasm, has made to my understanding and to this book. He also introduced me to Professor Arvind, vice chancellor of Punjab Agricultural University, Ludhiana, who took us to his own father, also a freedom fighter of Jhuggian's generation.

I am ever grateful to my friend Navsharan Singh in Delhi for introducing me to Kuldip and many, many others in Punjab, who made every journey of mine there worthwhile.

My sincere thanks to schoolteacher and local historian Ajmer Singh Sidhu. His inputs on the tragedy of Partition, his store of detail, lent depth to the Jhuggian story. And to

Swaraj Bir, editor of the *Punjabi Tribune*, who has always taken interest in my work and set up a fascinating meeting with author, lawyer and historian M. J. S. Waraich, whose knowledge of the revolutionary era is encyclopaedic.

My gratitude to Darshan Singh Mattu, a member of the CPI(M) Punjab State Committee and a long-time friend and comrade of Jhuggian. He handled some of the most pressing follow-ups on the story.

And I must acknowledge the encouragement of my old friend Professor Chaman Lal, who has dedicated decades of his life to introducing a new generation to the writings of Bhagat Singh.

Also, acknowledging Professor Ved Vatuk (ex-UC Berkeley) who, along with my friend, the late Maharaj Kaul, introduced me to the literature of the Ghadar Party. And took me for the first time to the Ghadar Memorial Hall in San Francisco. Both were major inspirations for me in this voyage.

My thanks to Antara Raman for her wonderful illustration of what Bhagat Singh Jhuggian's daring defiance at school in 1939 might have looked like. Also for designing the Freedom Fighter's Gallery on PARI—which readers can go to by scanning the QR codes at the end of each story.

And many, many thanks to my friend and fellow traveller Vishav Bharati, Special Correspondent, *The Tribune*, Chandigarh. There was almost no trip to Punjab and Chandigarh on this and other issues where Vishav was not there to introduce, interpret, translate and explain for me. Again, his network and range of contacts was and is formidable. As was his ability to always dig out things that I couldn't. Thank you, Vishav.

Bengaluru, Karnataka

This list of acknowledgements is also about my acknowledgement of many failures. H. S. Doreswamy was yet another wonderful freedom fighter waiting for this book. He died in May 2021, two months after our 5 March 2021 interview with him at his Jayanagar home in Bengaluru. That was the 104th year of his life.

Here was a man who had suffered COVID-19 and other illnesses—and was still ready to explain his positions to the media or spiritedly debate issues with his adversaries. At 102, he was still addressing public gatherings. A little over a month after our interview with him by his bedside—he had been unwell—on Ambedkar Jayanti, 14 April 2021, he presided over the online prize ceremony of the prestigious Spoorthidhama Awards (disclosure: I was the main awardee). What a human being!

My thanks and gratitude to Doreswamy's son D. Raju and daughter-in-law Chandrika Raju for their patience and explanations when I called them almost a year after his demise with many questions for the story on him in this book. My thanks also to Dr Vijaya, senior journalist and writer, who helped us arrange the main interview in the first place and helped in obtaining documents that went into the story's making.

My thanks again to PARI's Siddhita Sonavane and Pratishtha Pandya, who transcribed very difficult parts of the audio track in the video recordings of our interview with Doreswamy.

My deepest gratitude to my old friends and fellow travellers G. N. Mohan and Sreeja V. N. Again, there is no measuring what they've made possible for me in Karnataka. There is almost nothing I have done in that state in the past decade that has not been set up by the two of them—not just the interview with Doreswamy. But they set that one up as well, and Sreeja shot the video footage for it. Thanks also to my PARI colleague Priti David who joined us to help with the interview.

G. N. Mohan has been my friend, guide, translator (he both translated and published *Everybody Loves a Good Drought* in Kannada) and interpreter for over two decades. If I was able to do a lot of work in the state it was because of Mohan. Many, many thanks to both him and Sreeja.

Ajmer, Rajasthan

The day this book is out, the person I shall be calling on in gratitude and admiration is Shobharam Gehervar, the 96-year-old *swatantrata sainik* in Ajmer. And, of course, his sister Shanti. Shobharam's scathing wit and amazing articulation will always stay in my mind. What a life story. What a storyteller! Also, the simple and succinct way that he addressed some of the furious political debates and questions of our time was refreshing and educative. My thanks to him, and to Shanti and her family. Also to Shobharam's nephew Shyam Sundar, who told us of and took us to his uncle in Ajmer.

Many thanks to PARI's Medha Kale, who transcribed and translated the lengthy interview I did with Shobharam Gehervar in Ajmer. PARI's Urja, based in Udaipur, travelled with us to Ajmer and shot some excellent footage which will go up on our under-construction Freedom Fighters Gallery. And my thanks to Sarika Narayan, an infinitely patient 'auditor' for not just listening to the Shobharam story, but for many of the others as well.

None of the above would ever have happened if it were not for my old friend and colleague Kavita Srivastava of the People's Union for Civil Liberties. It was she who made my search for living freedom fighters in Rajasthan possible at all. And it was she who helped conduct the interview and made valuable inputs in it with her own questions. I did, however, miss the presence of the wonderful journalist, the late Neelabh Mishra, together with whom I had traversed very large tracts of Rajasthan over many years.

Chennai, Tamil Nadu

My gratitude to Comrade N. Sankariah in Chennai. Completely aside from authoring a book in which he figures, just the sheer experience of interacting with him is exhilarating. But yes, the stories of his adventures in the 1940s—and we marvelled during the interviews at his near-photographic memory—are gripping and real. He has no regrets over the years lost to imprisonment and is proud to have sacrificed them for his country.

My sincere thanks to him and his family, particularly to his son Comrade R. Narasimhan of the CPI(M).

So too, my gratitude to Comrade R. Nallakannu of the CPI. I cannot remember meeting a more self-effacing human being in recent years. Like his comrade of seven decades N. Sankariah, Comrade RNK's experiences are fascinating and told me much about the electoral and anti-feudal battles of the 1930s and 1940s that I had no knowledge of at all. My thanks to Comrade Uday Kumar of the CPI for all his assistance.

My sincere thanks to Comrade Nallakannu's family, particularly his granddaughter Priya for all her help. My thanks also to Comrade G. Ramakrishnan and Professor Venkatesh Athreya for their inputs on the RNK story.

The PARI team in Tamil Nadu is an extraordinary one, and they breathe energy into anything I do. Our genius photographer Palani Kumar went out in the middle of the lockdown to get me photos I needed from Madurai for the Sankariah story. Also part of that team—PARI's brilliant writer Aparna Karthikeyan, whose detailed response as an enthusiastic 'auditor' made me feel good about every word I wrote.

Palani Kumar shot hours and hours of flawless video in the main interviews. While also taking still photos in between. S. Gavaskar took some great photographs for us of the Sankariah and Nallakannu interviews. Many of these will be accessible to readers of this book via the QR codes at the end of each story. The page on PARI that the QR codes will take them to will in time include the videos, ably edited by Prabhu Manikandan. And my sincere thanks to Bharathy Singaravel and R. Shobhana for the huge efforts involved in transcribing and translating the videos. Also, many thanks to PARI's Rajasangeethan, who has translated so much of my work into Tamil and to Kavitha Gajendran for her help with that process. Pratishtha Pandya transcribed Comrade Sankariah's statements in a video interview (up on PARI) at great speed to help beat the story deadline.

The entire exercise in Tamil Nadu rested on the efforts of PARI's Kavitha Muralidharan, one of the finest journalists I know. I learnt a lot from her on how to approach the interviews with these freedom fighters. Organizing, setting up the coordination, overseeing the transcription and translation of the videos—and pulling off the coup of that final interview where we got both NS and RNK together in a chat about their times in the 1940s—all these things rested on her efforts. There is no way I can ever thank her enough.

To learn more about the foot soldiers of Indian freedom, visit the People's Archive of Rural India website at www.ruralindiaonline.org. Or scan the QR code below.